ESSENTIAL BIERCE

Spanaway Lake
High School

ESSENTIAL BIERCE

A selection of the writings of Ambrose Bierce

Edited with an Introduction by
JOHN R. DUNLAP

Spanaway Lake
High School

Santa Clara University, Santa Clara, California
Heyday Books, Berkeley, California

Introduction © 2007 by John R. Dunlap

Library of Congress Cataloging-in-Publication Data

Bierce, Ambrose, 1842-1914?
 [Selections. 2007]
 Essential Bierce : a selection of the writings of Ambrose Bierce / edited with
an introduction by John R. Dunlap.
    p. cm. -- (A California legacy book)
 Includes bibliographical references.
 ISBN 978-1-59714-054-6 (pbk. : alk. paper)
 I. Dunlap, John R., 1945- II. Title.
 PS1097.A6 2007
 813'.4--dc22
                                    2006039388

Cover Art and Design: Lorraine Rath
Interior Design: Philip Krayna, PKD, Berkeley
Typesetting: Lorraine Rath
Printing and Binding: Sheridan, Ann Arbor, MI

Orders, inquiries, and correspondence should be addressed to:
    Heyday Books
    P. O. Box 9145, Berkeley, CA 94709
    (510) 549-3564, Fax (510) 549-1889
    www.heydaybooks.com

Printed in the United States of America on 50% post consumer waste
recycled paper. ♻

10 9 8 7 6 5 4 3 2 1

To Terry Beers, for putting this bee in my bonnet

To Vicki and the kids, for putting up with it all

Contents

Introduction

Since his fabled disappearance in Mexico at the age of seventy-one in December 1913, the permanent allure of Ambrose Bierce (1842–1914?) has derived partly from his contradictions and anomalies. He despised organized religion with a kind of passion that most people disappointed in their religious upbringing get over after late adolescence, yet he confessed a warm respect for Mormons, Catholics, and Jews—and his own writing, especially the poetry, often nods wistfully to a transcendent order, without apparent irony. He treated the emerging women's movement of his era with a puzzled scorn, yet he assiduously encouraged the talent of hopeful women poets, and long after his death women writers and scholars (Gertrude Atherton, Bertha Clark Pope, M. E. Grenander) have been among his most ardent admirers. In lucid critical essays, he often condemned mediocrity in literature, appealing to the highest standards of artistic expression, yet he extolled the eccentric work of such middling literary figures as George Sterling and Herman Scheffauer.

Some, perhaps all of the apparent contradictions may, on a deeper level, be taken as perfectly consistent in a man of Bierce's unusual integrity. As a muckraking journalist, he was implacably and, at some personal risk, publicly hostile to California's bigwig politicos and robber barons (Leland Stanford, Charles Crocker, Mark Hopkins, Collis P. Huntington: the "Big Four" of the Central and Southern Pacific Railroads) and he favored state control of the railroads, yet he despised socialism, shook his journalistic fist at labor strikes, and, in his satire, roasted busybody reformers of any sort. He was a "reprehensibly" (his own term in a letter to a friend) inattentive husband and parent, yet the suicide of his sixteen-year-old son Day in 1889 (after a childish and murderous gunfight over a girl) plunged Bierce into a dark depression with which he labored through the most fiercely creative three years of his life, producing the bulk of his fictional masterpieces. He frequently exhibited a short fuse and disdained fussiness and tedium, yet his manners were fastidious and his correspondence faithful; in his last years, under contract with his publisher, he pulled together twelve volumes of his *Collected Works*—tracking down material, cutting, pasting, revising, and minutely attending to the many errors of a careless typesetter.

Born June 24, 1842, on a farm in Meiggs County, Ohio, Ambrose Gwinnett Bierce was the tenth of Marcus and Laura Bierce's thirteen children, and the youngest of those who survived to adulthood. The family moved to a farm in northern Indiana in 1846, where Bierce grew up with the companionship of his older brother Albert. (Marcus Aurelius Bierce, the father, had given all his children names beginning with A.) He read abundantly in his father's fairly stocked personal library and attended school in nearby Warsaw, a three-mile walk. From age fifteen to seventeen, he lived in Warsaw, working as a printer's devil for *The Northern Indianian*, an abolitionist newspaper. For a while he lived with an uncle, Lucius Verus Bierce, in Akron, Ohio. Uncle Lucius, a local politician, had been a flamboyant military adventurer full of wonderful stories, which apparently moved Bierce, in the fall of 1859, to enroll at the Kentucky Military Institute at Franklin Springs.

After a year at the Institute—where he studied draftsmanship and cartography as well as Latin, English grammar, history, and mathematics—he dropped out and returned to Indiana. He settled into an aimless existence for the next nine months in Elkhart, a town thirty miles north of Warsaw, working odd jobs and frequently traveling down to Warsaw to visit with a school sweetheart, Bernice Wright, and her sister Clara. News of the outbreak of the

Civil War at Fort Sumter in April 1861 dispelled his lassitude (a frame of mind he was to drift into with some regularity in subsequent years; in today's therapeutic culture Bierce would probably be regarded as "clinically depressed"), and in the following month, at age eighteen, Bierce enlisted for a three-month stint with the Ninth Indiana Volunteers.

The volunteer regiment saw action in West Virginia at Philippi on June 3, and Bierce's first of several heroic exploits occurred the following month at Laurel Hill, where, under withering Confederate fire, he carried a fatally wounded corporal more than a hundred yards to cover. When the brief stint with the Ninth was over, the nineteen-year-old Bierce reenlisted with the rank of sergeant in August 1861. Within a month he was advanced to the rank of sergeant major, and in February 1862 his regiment, assigned to the Army of the Ohio, joined Colonel William B. Hazen's 19th Brigade of the army's Fourth Division at Nashville.

From that point on, Bierce was in the thick of it: Shiloh, Stones River, Chickamauga, the siege of Chattanooga, the Union charge at Missionary Ridge, the appalling Atlanta campaign. Colonel Hazen, alert to the talent and daring of the young sergeant major, had attached Bierce to his staff with the rank of second lieutenant. Apart from his valor, Bierce's brief training at the Kentucky Military Institute had given him skills in surveying and mapmaking, which his superiors depended upon in anticipation of battle; the job as "topographical engineer," of course, was perilous as well as crucial, and Bierce was soon advanced to the rank of first lieutenant.

After several brushes with death over a harrowing two years, his luck almost ran out on June 23, 1864, when, leading forward a skirmish line at Kennesaw Mountain (a movement Hazen later described as gallant but unnecessary), Bierce was felled by a shot to the head. By an extreme fluke (head wounds being nearly always fatal in the Civil War), the bullet struck Bierce in the left temple, burrowed obliquely a few inches, and lodged behind his ear without penetrating the skull. Hospitalized in Chattanooga, Bierce was sent home on convalescent leave in July, where, for reasons unknown, he broke off his engagement with Bernice Wright. He returned to less hazardous duty in September, but resigned on grounds of physical disability (in addition to bouts with asthma, he was to suffer intermittent headaches for the rest of his life) in January 1865. Before his discharge, however, he accompanied Sherman on the exhausting fifty-day march from Savannah to Goldsboro; he was released from service shortly before Lee's surrender at Appomattox. His military service from the start to the finish of the Civil War was later to give Bierce the haunting material for his fictional masterpieces and such stunning recollections as "What I Saw of Shiloh."

The war years also set in motion a sequence of events that brought Ambrose Bierce to California. After a brief and somewhat dangerous stint as a Treasury agent in the reconstructing South, Bierce jumped at the opportunity to accompany his friend and former commanding officer, now Brigadier General William Hazen, on an inspection tour of western military forts, which took him from Omaha to Sacramento on horseback. He was seriously considering a career in the Army when, in 1867, the inspection party arrived in San Francisco by ferry from Sacramento, but when a message from Washington offered him the rank of second lieutenant (he had mustered out two years earlier as a first lieutenant, and anticipated the rank of captain if he returned to the Army), Bierce decided on civilian life with the thought of becoming a writer.

Taking work as a guard at the U.S. Mint in San Francisco, Bierce amused his co-workers with his rants against organized religion, and set about doggedly to hone his skills as a writer. He read widely and deeply, and pored over *Webster's Unabridged Dictionary.* (Some traces of his mood and regimen can be spotted in his essay "To Train a Writer," included in this volume.) He submitted his work successfully to such publications as *Californian* and *Golden Era,* and by December 1868 he was a regular columnist ("The Town Crier") for the *San Francisco News Letter.* His reputation spreading quickly, he contributed now and then to Bret Harte's *Overland Monthly,* where he first published a short story, "The Haunted

Valley," in 1871. In December of that year Bierce was wed to Mary Ellen ("Mollie") Day, the daughter of a wealthy mining engineer. He celebrated their lengthy courtship in his charming poem "To Thee, My Darling":

The heliotrope's fragrant breath—
The subtle sweet of jasmine on the evening air—
The flowery mead, all radiant
With sympathetic pleasure
From the glowing kiss with which
The God of Day salutes its lovely face—
The whispering, snowy surf, wherewith
Old Ocean in his kindliest mood
Murmurs soft secrets to the willing sands—
The mingled joy and anguish thrilling us
In the weird plaints of Schubert—
Great Rossini's heaven-born strains—
All graceful, lovely things,
Lifting my soul to beatific state,—
Mnemosyne with flowery fetters
Binds to thee, my darling.

The newlyweds took up residence across the bay in San Rafael, at the time a summer resort, partly because of Bierce's chronic asthma, which foggy San Francisco was never kind to. The residence was short-lived, however. Bierce, enticed by reports from Joaquin Miller and letters from London where his Town Crier column was avidly read, resigned from the *News Letter* in March 1872 in preparation for a trip to England. With financial backing from Bierce's wealthy father-in-law, the couple left for London in the summer.

Bierce, an inveterate anglophile, later referred to the three years he spent in England as the happiest in his life. Already much admired in London, he quickly developed cozy relations with an assortment of journalistic cronies and drinking buddies. He wrote stories for Tom Hood's satiric magazine *Fun* and regular columns for *Figaro*. He published three book-length collections of his work. Meanwhile, however, the London climate was no gentler on Bierce's asthma than San Francisco's had been, so that Ambrose and Mollie moved frequently during their time in England: from London to Bristol (where their first son, Day, was born in December 1872) to Bath, back to London, back to Bath, and finally to Leamington, in Warwickshire, where their second son, Leigh, was born in April 1874.

The frequent moving and a lengthy visit from Bierce's intrusive mother-in-law, not to mention Bierce's preoccupation with his writing and with the company of his London pals, did not bode well for the marriage. Pregnant again and homesick, Mollie returned to San Francisco with her toddler sons in April 1875. Bierce reluctantly followed in September, just before their daughter, Helen, was born the following month. To make ends meet, he took up work in the assay office of the U.S. Mint and, in March 1877, landed a position as associate editor and columnist ("The Prattler") for a new magazine, *Argonaut.*

His growing family, however, and the disturbing prospect of dependence on his rich father-in-law nudged Bierce into thinking seriously about earning money. In the assay office, mindful of his father-in-law's success as a mining engineer, Bierce had become fascinated with gold mining ventures in the Black Hills of the Dakota Territory. After careful study of the possibilities, he resigned from *Argonaut* and, in 1880, secured the position of general agent for the Black Hills Placer Mining Company, a huge New York corporation with plans to build a dam and a seventeen-mile wooden flume to carry water from Spring Creek to the town of Rockerville, Dakota Territory, a place rich with otherwise inaccessible gold deposits. Leaving Mollie and the kids in California, Bierce traveled to Rockerville to oversee a project already mired in mismanagement and the dangerously ill will of unpaid workers and contractors. Bierce exhibited remarkable business skills and honesty in what turned out to be a hopeless effort to correct the mismanagement. In October he resigned and traveled to New York, where he spent two months defending himself against false allegations from corrupt and incompetent former managers.

Bierce apparently had planned to settle with his family in Rockerville when the flume was completed and the rich deposits of gold could start being washed from the soil. He never talked much about this acutely disappointing episode in his life, partly because of the legal wrangling that dragged on for years before a settlement slightly in his favor, but he acquired huge reserves of material to shape his hilariously stinging views of the legal profession. In January 1881 he returned to San Francisco and joined the staff of the weekly *Wasp*, a satirical newspaper. He resumed his "Prattler" column and started publishing serial installments of *The Devil's Dictionary*. Having brushed up all too closely against the abrasive underside of big business, Bierce now launched his relentless attacks against the Central and Southern Pacific Railroads, whose corrupt minions dominated state politics. But *Wasp* was troubled by a vacillating ownership, and Bierce resigned in 1886. The paper folded shortly thereafter. In March of the following year, Bierce's future suddenly brightened when he was invited personally by a youthful William Randolph Hearst to accept the well-paid job of chief editorial writer for the *San Francisco Examiner*.

Bierce's tenure at the *Examiner*, from 1887 to his resignation in 1906, marks the most productive period of his life. The Sunday edition of the *Examiner* became the venue for the publication of his occasional stories, including most of his masterpieces. His best essays first appeared (or appeared in substantially revised form from previously published drafts) in the *Examiner*. He continued his installments of *The Devil's Dictionary*, and produced the most significant and enduring of his journalistic broadsides—although he also continued to misjudge literary talent with, for example, a dismissal of Stephen Crane as a "freak."

In January 1896, Hearst sent Bierce to Washington to monitor (and hound and lobby against) a funding bill before Congress that would effectively have forgiven the railroad magnate Collis P. Huntington some $25 million in debts to the U.S. government for loans advanced to Huntington for railroad construction. From January to June, Bierce flailed away at the preposterous Huntington in more than sixty news articles laced with vitriol, driving the hapless robber baron to an attempted bribe, which Bierce shrugged off. The bill was defeated in June, but Bierce stayed in the East until November, first in Gettysburg and then in New York, where his son

Leigh (who had accompanied Bierce on the trip back east) was now working as a reporter for the New York *Morning Journal*, a recent Hearst acquisition.

Bierce had found his stay in Washington exciting and agreeable, and many of his closest friends now lived in the East. There were many reasons too for Bierce to feel disaffected with California. Never a very attentive husband, he had separated from his wife Mollie late in 1888 on a flimsy pretext of jealousy. In the following year, he was unnerved by the suicide of his oldest son Day, who, at age sixteen, shot himself to death after killing his best friend in a gun duel over a girl in Chico. By the middle of the 1890s, Bierce's closest friends were either dead or had moved, and he was getting bored with his own writing. One may suppose as well that Bierce's frequent changes of residence in California to relieve his chronic asthma were starting to wear on him: San Rafael, St. Helena, Auburn, Sunol, Berkeley, Oakland, San Jose, Los Gatos, the Santa Cruz mountains.

Back in San Francisco after the triumph over Huntington, Bierce continued publishing stories in the *Examiner*, and in 1898 produced a series of articles on the Spanish-American War. This time, however, Bierce stood against the editorial position of the *Examiner* and of Hearst himself. An early exponent of isolationism, Bierce thought the war bogus and the imperial reach ridiculous and needlessly dangerous.

Hearst—partly, perhaps, because he was so preoccupied with his own political projects—never troubled Bierce about his disagreements with the *Examiner*. When Bierce moved permanently to Washington in 1899, he joined the press corps in the Capitol and continued writing for the *Examiner* and, later, for Hearst's newly acquired magazine *Cosmopolitan*, where he published several more of his stories. As he anticipated, Bierce found Washington to his liking. Generally sociable despite the public image of lone curmudgeon, he was happy to join the Army and Navy Club, where he could hobnob with active duty officers and fellow veterans, sporting his honorary rank of major, with which he had been brevetted years earlier for his distinguished war record. Among other reasons for the move to Washington, Bierce wanted to be closer to his son

Leigh, who had stayed in New York and had helped Bierce with some publishing projects.

After losing Day, Bierce was careful to stay in touch with his surviving son and, as well, his daughter, Helen. But Leigh—a compulsive womanizer and severe alcoholic—died of pneumonia (the result of a drinking bender) in March 1901 with a distraught Bierce at his son's bedside. Bierce had made some feeble efforts to dissuade Leigh from the young man's dissolute habits, yet he was sensible enough to know that he had no one to blame but himself if his word carried little authority with his children. Leigh's death, at age twenty-six, sank Bierce into a lengthy funk of depression and self-recrimination. Within a year of the loss, his sandy blonde hair had turned white.

In the same year, though, Bierce became acquainted with Walter Neale, a young publisher who eventually set up shop in New York. Neale—although a self-styled Virginia "aristocrat" and something of an operator—was nonetheless a reliable and honest businessman, unlike several earlier publishers Bierce had dealt with. Bierce enjoyed Neale's energetic company, and Neale greatly admired Bierce's writing, eventually persuading him to undertake the four-year labor of pulling together his *Collected Works*, at first planned for ten volumes but finally expanded to twelve. During his Washington years, Bierce also completed his *Devil's Dictionary* and published his less-well-known lexicon, *Write It Right*, a seventy-three-page alphabetized usage guide, the short preface to which ("Aims and the Plan," included here) is a neat statement of Bierce's theory of style.

By early 1913, when Bierce had finished his *Collected Works*, he might well have faded into a cozy retirement, but he had other plans. For several months, with the help of Carrie Christensen, his personal secretary, he settled his legal and financial affairs, often expressing his intent of traveling to revolution-torn Mexico and then to South America. On a last visit with his daughter in Bloomington, Illinois, Bierce left in her care a large collection of private papers and documents. Helen later recalled her father's being distracted during the visit. One evening Bierce and his daughter were sitting on the front porch in quiet conversation. The seventy-one-year-old Bierce nodded towards a decrepit-looking old man shuffling by on the sidewalk and said, "I'll never be like that."

He never was. In October, Bierce left Washington for New Orleans, stopping along the way to visit the Civil War battlefields of his youth. He stayed in New Orleans a few days, where he was interviewed by reporters, and then headed for San Antonio, Texas, where he stayed just over a week, somewhat incapacitated by his asthma, which was flaring up intermittently during the trip. Continuing the journey, he arrived in Laredo on November 7, where he was feted by admiring soldiers at Fort McIntosh. From Laredo, Bierce traveled to El Paso, whence he entered Mexico in mid-November. His last surviving letter, dated December 26, places him in Chihuahua, heading for "an unknown destination." Thereafter Bierce disappears.

The disappearance thus far has inspired almost a century of recurring speculation and uncertain investigation. What did Ambrose Bierce do, or what happened to him, in Mexico? The best survey of the speculation, with informed and sensibly deductive measures of plausibility, can be found in Roy Morris Jr.'s recent biography, *Ambrose Bierce: Alone in Bad Company* (Oxford, 1995, pp. 249–68). The guesswork includes a strong case for suicide, not to mention a breathtaking, if inadvertent, display of Bierce's adroit manipulation of his own image.

Yet, as Morris and others have suggested, we honor Bierce today with the question mark after his death year (1914?). It suits the man neatly. Through most of his remarkable life, for better or for worse, Ambrose Bierce favored the sharp edges of wit over the rounded contours of sustained reflection, and the best wit takes us by surprise. The question mark is an apt conclusion to that life. Mysterious, unsettling, reliably Biercean.

Stories

Bierce's 90-plus short stories divide easily into three categories: tales of horror, tales of war, and tall tales. He was a master at depicting the startling landscape—whether an evocative scene, or the topology of a character's tormented mind, or a finely chiseled piece of dialogue. His oft-repeated dismissal of the novel as a "barren art" and a dying literary form (see, for example, his essay on "The Novel," in *Collected Works*, X, 17–24) may owe something to his own limitations. He seems to have lacked the ability as well as the inclination to paint on a large canvas. His preoccupation in his fiction (and elsewhere, for that matter) was always, in Bertha Clark Pope's phrase (*Letters*, xviii), "the one decisive moment of crisis."

The Haunted Valley

I

How Trees Are Felled in China

A half-mile north from Jo. Dunfer's, on the road from Hutton's to Mexican Hill, the highway dips into a sunless ravine which opens out on either hand in a half-confidential manner, as if it had a secret to impart at some more convenient season. I never used to ride through it without looking first to the one side and then to the other, to see if the time had arrived for the revelation. If I saw nothing—and I never did see anything—there was no feeling of disappointment, for I knew the disclosure was merely withheld temporarily for some good reason which I had no right to question. That I should one day be taken into full confidence I no more doubted than I doubted the existence of Jo. Dunfer himself, through whose premises the ravine ran.

It was said that Jo. had once undertaken to erect a cabin in some remote part of it, but for some reason had abandoned the enterprise and constructed his present hermaphrodite habitation, half residence and half groggery, at the roadside, upon an extreme corner of his estate; as far away as possible, as if on purpose to show how radically he had changed his mind.

This Jo. Dunfer—or, as he was familiarly known in the neighborhood, Whisky Jo.—was a very important personage in those parts. He was apparently about forty years of age, a long, shockheaded fellow, with a corded face, a gnarled arm and a knotty hand like a bunch of prison-keys. He was a hairy man, with a stoop in his

3

walk, like that of one who is about to spring upon something and rend it.

Next to the peculiarity to which he owed his local appellation, Mr. Dunfer's most obvious characteristic was a deep-seated antipathy to the Chinese. I saw him once in a towering rage because one of his herdsmen had permitted a travel-heated Asian to slake his thirst at the horse-trough in front of the saloon end of Jo.'s establishment. I ventured faintly to remonstrate with Jo. for his unchristian spirit, but he merely explained that there was nothing about Chinamen in the New Testament, and strode away to wreak his displeasure upon his dog, which also, I suppose, the inspired scribes had overlooked.

Some days afterward, finding him sitting alone in his barroom, I cautiously approached the subject, when, greatly to my relief, the habitual austerity of his expression visibly softened into something that I took for condescension.

"You young Easterners," he said, "are a mile-and-a-half too good for this country, and you don't catch on to our play. People who don't know a Chileño from a Kanaka can afford to hang out liberal ideas about Chinese immigration, but a fellow that has to fight for his bone with a lot of mongrel coolies hasn't any time for foolishness."

This long consumer, who had probably never done an honest day's-work in his life, sprung the lid of a Chinese tobacco-box and with thumb and forefinger forked out a wad like a small haycock. Holding this reinforcement within supporting distance he fired away with renewed confidence.

"They're a flight of devouring locusts, and they're going for everything green in this God blest land, if you want to know."

Here he pushed his reserve into the breach and when his gabble-gear was again disengaged resumed his uplifting discourse.

"I had one of them on this ranch five years ago, and I'll tell you about it, so that you can see the nub of this whole question. I didn't pan out particularly well those days—drank more whisky than was prescribed for me and didn't seem to care for my duty as a patriotic American citizen; so I took that pagan in, as a kind of cook. But when I got religion over at the Hill and they talked of running me for the Legislature it was given to me to see the light. But what was I to do? If I gave him the go somebody else would take him, and mightn't treat him white. *What* was I to do? What would any good Christian do, especially one new to the trade and full to the neck with the brotherhood of Man and the fatherhood of God?"

Jo. paused for a reply, with an expression of unstable satisfaction, as of one who has solved a problem by a distrusted method. Presently he rose and swallowed a glass of whisky from a full bottle on the counter, then resumed his story.

"Besides, he didn't count for much—didn't know anything and gave himself airs. They all do that. I said him nay, but he muled it through on that line while he lasted; but after turning the other cheek seventy and seven times I doctored the dice so that he didn't last forever. And I'm almighty glad I had the sand to do it."

Jo.'s gladness, which somehow did not impress me, was duly and ostentatiously celebrated at the bottle.

"About five years ago I started in to stick up a shack. That was before this one was built, and I put it in another place. I set Ah Wee and a little cuss named Gopher to cutting the timber. Of course I didn't expect Ah Wee to help much, for he had a face like a day in June and big black eyes—I guess maybe they were the damn'dest eyes in this neck o' woods."

While delivering this trenchant thrust at common sense Mr. Dunfer absently regarded a knot-hole in the thin board partition separating the bar from the living-room, as if that were one of the eyes whose size and color had incapacitated his servant for good service.

"Now you Eastern galoots won't believe anything against the yellow devils," he suddenly flamed out with an appearance of earnestness not altogether convincing, "but I tell you that Chink was the perversest scoundrel outside San Francisco. The miserable pig-tail Mongolian went to hewing away at the saplings all round the stems, like a worm o' the dust gnawing a radish. I pointed out his error as patiently as I knew how, and showed him how to cut them on two sides, so as to make them fall right; but no sooner would I turn my back on him, like this"—and he turned it on me, amplifying the illustration by taking some more liquor—"than he was at it again. It was just this way: while I looked at him, *so*"—regarding me rather unsteadily and with evident complexity of vision—"he was all right; but when I looked away, *so*"—taking a long pull at the bottle—"he defied me. Then I'd gaze at him reproachfully, *so*, and butter wouldn't have melted in his mouth."

Doubtless Mr. Dunfer honestly intended the look that he fixed upon me to be merely reproachful, but it was singularly fit to arouse the gravest apprehension in any unarmed person incurring it; and as I had lost all interest in his pointless and interminable narrative, I rose to go. Before I had fairly risen, he had again turned to the counter, and with a barely audible "so," had emptied the bottle at a gulp.

Heavens! what a yell! It was like a Titan in his last, strong agony. Jo. staggered back after emitting it, as a cannon recoils from its own thunder, and then dropped into his chair, as if he had been "knocked in the head" like a beef—his eyes drawn sidewise toward the wall, with a stare of terror. Looking in the same direction, I saw that the knot-hole in the wall had indeed become a human eye—a full, black eye, that glared into my own with an entire lack of expression more awful than the most devilish glitter. I think I must have covered my face with my hands to shut out the horrible illusion, if such it was, and Jo.'s little white man-of-all-work coming into the room broke the spell, and I walked out of the house with a sort of dazed fear that *delirium tremens* might be infectious. My horse was hitched at the watering-trough, and untying him I mounted and gave him his head, too much troubled in mind to note whither he took me.

I did not know what to think of all this, and like every one who does not know what to think I thought a great deal, and to little purpose. The only reflection that seemed at all satisfactory, was, that on the morrow I should be some miles away, with a strong probability of never returning.

A sudden coolness brought me out of my abstraction, and looking up I found myself entering the deep shadows of the ravine. The day was stifling; and this transition from the pitiless, visible heat of the parched fields to the cool gloom, heavy with pungency of cedars and vocal with twittering of the birds that had been driven to its leafy asylum, was exquisitely refreshing. I looked for my mystery, as usual, but not finding the ravine in a communicative mood, dismounted, led my sweating animal into the undergrowth, tied him securely to a tree and sat down upon a rock to meditate.

I began bravely by analyzing my pet superstition about the place. Having resolved it into its constituent elements I arranged them in convenient troops and squadrons, and collecting all the forces of my logic bore down upon them from impregnable premises with the thunder of irresistible conclusions and a great noise of chariots and general intellectual shouting. Then, when my big mental guns had overturned all opposition, and were growling almost inaudibly away on the horizon of pure speculation, the routed enemy straggled in upon their rear, massed silently into a solid phalanx, and captured me, bag and baggage. An indefinable dread came upon me. I rose to shake it off, and began threading the narrow dell by an old, grass-grown cow-path that seemed to flow along the bottom, as a substitute for the brook that Nature had neglected to provide.

The trees among which the path straggled were ordinary, well-behaved plants, a trifle perverted as to trunk and eccentric as to bough, but with nothing unearthly in their general aspect. A few loose bowlders, which had detached themselves from the sides of the depression to set up an independent existence at the bottom, had dammed up the pathway, here and there, but their stony repose had nothing in it of the stillness of death. There was a kind of death-chamber hush in the valley, it is true, and a mysterious whisper above: the wind was just fingering the tops of the trees—that was all.

I had not thought of connecting Jo. Dunfer's drunken narrative with what I now sought, and only when I came into a clear space and stumbled over the level trunks of some small trees did I have the revelation. This was the site of the abandoned "shack." The discovery was verified by noting that some of the rotting stumps were hacked all round, in a most unwoodmanlike way, while others were cut straight across, and the butt ends of the corresponding trunks had the blunt wedge-form given by the axe of a master.

The opening among the trees was not more than thirty paces across. At one side was a little knoll—a natural hillock, bare of shrubbery but covered with wild grass, and on this, standing out of the grass, the headstone of a grave!

I do not remember that I felt anything like surprise at this discovery. I viewed that lonely grave with something of the feeling that Columbus must have had when he saw the hills and headlands of the new world. Before approaching it I leisurely completed my survey of the surroundings. I was even guilty of the affectation of winding my watch at that unusual hour, and with needless care and deliberation. Then I approached my mystery.

The grave—a rather short one—was in somewhat better repair than was consistent with its obvious age and isolation, and my eyes, I dare say, widened a trifle at a clump of unmistakable garden flowers showing evidence of recent watering. The stone had clearly enough done duty once as a doorstep. In its front was carved, or rather dug, an inscription. It read thus:

> AH WEE—CHINAMAN.
> Age unknown. Worked for Jo. Dunfer.
> This monument is erected by him to keep the Chink's
> memory green. Likewise as a warning to Celestials
> not to take on airs. Devil take 'em!
> She Was a Good Egg.

I cannot adequately relate my astonishment at this uncommon inscription! The meagre but sufficient identification of the deceased; the impudent candor of confession; the brutal anathema; the ludicrous change of sex and sentiment—all marked this record as the work of one who must have been at least as much demented as bereaved. I felt that any further disclosure would be a paltry anticlimax, and with an unconscious regard for dramatic effect turned squarely about and walked away. Nor did I return to that part of the county for four years.

II

Who Drives Sane Oxen Should Himself Be Sane

"Gee-up, there, old Fuddy-Duddy!"

This unique adjuration came from the lips of a queer little man perched upon a wagonful of firewood, behind a brace of oxen that were hauling it easily along with a simulation of mighty effort which had evidently not imposed on their lord and master. As that gentleman happened at the moment to be staring me squarely in the face as I stood by the roadside it was not altogether clear whether he was addressing me or his beasts; nor could I say if they were named Fuddy and Duddy and were both subjects of the imperative verb "to gee-up." Anyhow the command produced no effect on us, and the queer little man removed his eyes from mine long enough to spear Fuddy and Duddy alternately with a long pole, remarking, quietly but with feeling: "Dern your skin," as if they enjoyed that integument in common. Observing that my request for a ride took no attention, and finding myself falling slowly astern, I placed one foot upon the inner circumference of a hind wheel and was slowly elevated to the level of the hub, whence I boarded the concern, *sans cérémonie,* and scrambling forward seated myself beside the driver—who took no notice of me until he had administered another indiscriminate castigation to his cattle, accompanied with the advice to "buckle down, you derned Incapable!" Then, the master of the outfit (or rather the former master, for I could not suppress a whimsical feeling that the entire establishment was my lawful prize) trained his big, black eyes upon me with an expression strangely, and somewhat unpleasantly, familiar, laid down his rod—which neither blossomed nor turned into a serpent, as I half expected—folded his arms, and gravely demanded, "W'at did you do to W'isky?"

My natural reply would have been that I drank it, but there was something about the query that suggested a hidden significance, and something about the man that did not invite a shallow jest. And so, having no other answer ready, I merely held my tongue, but felt as if I were resting under an imputation of guilt, and that my silence was being construed into a confession.

Just then a cold shadow fell upon my cheek, and caused me to look up. We were descending into my ravine! I can not describe the sensation that came upon me: I had not seen it since it unbosomed itself four years before, and now I felt like one to whom a friend has made some sorrowing confession of crime long past, and who has basely deserted him in consequence. The old memories of Jo. Dunfer, his fragmentary revelation, and the unsatisfying

explanatory note by the headstone, came back with singular distinctness. I wondered what had become of Jo., and—I turned
sharply round and asked my prisoner. He was intently watching his
cattle, and without withdrawing his eyes replied:

"Gee-up, old Terrapin! He lies aside of Ah Wee up the gulch. Like
to see it? They always come back to the spot—I've been expectin'
you. H-woa!"

At the enunciation of the aspirate, Fuddy-Duddy, the incapable
terrapin, came to a dead halt, and before the vowel had died away
up the ravine had folded up all his eight legs and lain down in the
dusty road, regardless of the effect upon his derned skin. The queer
little man slid off his seat to the ground and started up the dell
without deigning to look back to see if I was following. But I was.

It was about the same season of the year, and at near the same
hour of the day, of my last visit. The jays clamored loudly, and the
trees whispered darkly, as before; and I somehow traced in the two
sounds a fanciful analogy to the open boastfulness of Mr. Jo.
Dunfer's mouth and the mysterious reticence of his manner, and to
the mingled hardihood and tenderness of his sole literary produc-
tion—the epitaph. All things in the valley seemed unchanged,
excepting the cow-path, which was almost wholly overgrown with
weeds. When we came out into the "clearing," however, there was
change enough. Among the stumps and trunks of the fallen
saplings, those that had been hacked "China fashion" were no
longer distinguishable from those that were cut "'Melican way." It
was as if the Old-World barbarism and the New-World civilization
had reconciled their differences by the arbitration of an impartial
decay—as is the way of civilizations. The knoll was there, but the
Hunnish brambles had overrun and all but obliterated its effete
grasses; and the patrician garden-violet had capitulated to his
plebeian brother—perhaps had merely reverted to his original
type. Another grave—a long, robust mound—had been made
beside the first, which seemed to shrink from the comparison; and
in the shadow of a new headstone the old one lay prostrate, with its
marvelous inscription illegible by accumulation of leaves and soil.
In point of literary merit the new was inferior to the old—was even
repulsive in its terse and savage jocularity:

JO. DUNFER. DONE FOR.

I turned from it with indifference, and brushing away the leaves from the tablet of the dead pagan restored to light the mocking words which, fresh from their long neglect, seemed to have a certain pathos. My guide, too, appeared to take on an added seriousness as he read it, and I fancied that I could detect beneath his whimsical manner something of manliness, almost of dignity. But while I looked at him his former aspect, so subtly unhuman, so tantalizingly familiar, crept back into his big eyes, repellant and attractive. I resolved to make an end of the mystery if possible.

"My friend," I said, pointing to the smaller grave, "did Jo. Dunfer murder that Chinaman?"

He was leaning against a tree and looking across the open space into the top of another, or into the blue sky beyond. He neither withdrew his eyes, nor altered his posture as he slowly replied:

"No, sir; he justifiably homicided him."

"Then he really did kill him."

"Kill 'im? I should say he did, rather. Doesn't everybody know that? Didn't he stan' up before the coroner's jury and confess it? And didn't they find a verdict of 'Came to 'is death by a wholesome Christian sentiment workin' in the Caucasian breast'? An' didn't the church at the Hill turn W'isky down for it? And didn't the sovereign people elect him justice of the Peace to get even on the gospelers? I don't know where you were brought up."

"But did Jo. do that because the Chinaman did not, or would not, learn to cut down trees like a white man?"

"Sure!—it stan's so on the record, which makes it true an' legal. My knowin' better doesn't make any difference with legal truth; it wasn't my funeral and I wasn't invited to deliver an oration. But the fact is, W'isky was jealous o' *me*"—and the little wretch actually swelled out like a turkeycock and made a pretense of adjusting an imaginary neck-tie, noting the effect in the palm of his hand, held up before him to represent a mirror.

"Jealous of *you*!" I repeated with ill-mannered astonishment.

"That's what I said. Why not?—don't I look all right?"

He assumed a mocking attitude of studied grace, and twitched

the wrinkles out of his threadbare waistcoat. Then, suddenly dropping his voice to a low pitch of singular sweetness, he continued:

"W'isky thought a lot o' that Chink; nobody but me knew how
'e doted on 'im. Couldn't bear 'im out of 'is sight, the derned proto-
plasm! And w'en 'e came down to this clearin' one day an' found
him an' me neglectin' our work—him asleep an' me grapplin a
tarantula out of 'is sleeve—W'isky laid hold of my axe and let us
have it, good an' hard! I dodged just then, for the spider bit me, but
Ah Wee got it bad in the side an' tumbled about like anything.
W'isky was just weighin' me out one w'en 'e saw the spider fastened
on my finger; then 'e knew he'd made a jack ass of 'imself. He threw
away the axe and got down on 'is knees alongside of Ah Wee, who
gave a last little kick and opened 'is eyes—he had eyes like mine—
an' puttin' up 'is hands drew down W'isky's ugly head and held it
there w'ile 'e stayed. That wasn't long, for a tremblin' ran through
'im and 'e gave a bit of a moan an' beat the game."

During the progress of the story the narrator had become transfig-
ured. The comic, or rather, the sardonic element was all out of him, and
as he painted that strange scene it was with difficulty that I kept my
composure. And this consummate actor had somehow so managed me
that the sympathy due to his *dramatis personae* was given to himself. I
stepped forward to grasp his hand, when suddenly a broad grin danced
across his face and with a light, mocking laugh he continued:

"W'en W'isky got 'is nut out o' that 'e was a sight to see! All his
fine clothes—he dressed mighty blindin' those days—were spoiled
everlastin'! 'Is hair was towsled and his face—what I could see of it
was whiter than the ace of lilies. 'E stared once at me, and looked
away as if I didn't count; an' then there were shootin' pains chasin'
one another from my bitten finger into my head, and it was Gopher
to the dark. That's why I wasn't at the inquest."

"But why did you hold your tongue afterward?" I asked.

"It's that kind of tongue," he replied, and not another word
would he say about it.

"After that W'isky took to drinkin' harder an' harder, and was
rabider an' rabider anti-coolie, but I don't think 'e was ever particularly glad that 'e dispelled Ah Wee. He didn't put on so much dog
about it w'en we were alone as wen he had the ear of a derned

Spectacular Extravaganza like you. 'E put up that headstone and
gouged the inscription accordin' to his varyin' moods. It took 'im
three weeks, workin' between drinks. I gouged his in one day."
    "When did Jo. die?" I asked rather absently. The answer took my
breath:
    "Pretty soon after I looked at him through that knot-hole, w'en
you had put something in his w'isky, you derned Borgia!"
    Recovering somewhat from my surprise at this astounding
charge, I was half-minded to throttle the audacious accuser, but was
restrained by a sudden conviction that came to me in the light of a
revelation. I fixed a grave look upon him and asked, as calmly as I
could: "And when did you go luny?"
    "Nine years ago!" he shrieked, throwing out his clenched
hands—"nine years ago, w'en that big brute killed the woman who
loved him better than she did me!—me who had followed 'er from
San Francisco, where 'e won 'er at draw poker!—me who had
watched over 'er for years w'en the scoundrel she belonged to was
ashamed to acknowledge 'er and treat 'er white!—me who for her
sake kept 'is cussed secret till it ate 'im up!—me who w'en you poi-
soned the beast fulfilled 'is last request to lay 'im alongside 'er and
give 'im a stone to the head of 'im! And I've never since seen 'er
grave till now, for I didn't want to meet 'im here."
    "Meet him? Why, Gopher, my poor fellow, he is dead!"
    "That's why I'm afraid of 'im."
    I followed the little wretch back to his wagon and wrung his
hand at parting. It was now nightfall, and as I stood there at the
roadside in the deepening gloom, watching the blank outlines of
the receding wagon, a sound was borne to me on the evening
wind—a sound as of a series of vigorous thumps—and a voice
came out of the night:
    "Gee-up, there, you derned old Geranium."

A Watcher by the Dead

I

In an upper room of an unoccupied dwelling in the part of San Francisco known as North Beach lay the body of a man, under a sheet. The hour was near nine in the evening; the room was dimly lighted by a single candle. Although the weather was warm, the two windows, contrary to the custom which gives the dead plenty of air, were closed and the blinds drawn down. The furniture of the room consisted of but three pieces—an arm-chair, a small reading-stand supporting the candle, and a long kitchen table, supporting the body of the man. All these, as also the corpse, seemed to have been recently brought in, for an observer, had there been one, would have seen that all were free from dust, whereas everything else in the room was pretty thickly coated with it, and there were cobwebs in the angles of the walls.

Under the sheet the outlines of the body could be traced, even the features, these having that unnaturally sharp definition which seems to belong to faces of the dead, but is really characteristic of those only that have been wasted by disease. From the silence of the room one would rightly have inferred that it was not in the front of the house, facing a street. It really faced nothing but a high breast of rock, the rear of the building being set into a hill.

As a neighboring church clock was striking nine with an indolence which seemed to imply such an indifference to the flight of time that one could hardly help wondering why it took the trouble to strike at all, the single door of the room was opened and a man entered, advancing toward the body. As he did so the door closed, apparently of its own volition; there was a grating, as of a key turned with difficulty, and the snap of the lock bolt as it shot into its socket. A sound of retiring footsteps in the passage outside ensued, and the man was to all appearance a prisoner. Advancing to the table, he stood a moment looking down at the body; then with a slight shrug of the shoulders walked over to one of the windows and hoisted the blind. The darkness outside was absolute, the panes were covered with dust, but by wiping this away he could see that the window was fortified with strong iron bars crossing it within a few inches of the glass and imbedded in the masonry on each side. He examined the other window. It was the same. He manifested no great curiosity in the matter, did not even so much as raise the sash. If he was a prisoner he was apparently a tractable one. Having completed his examination of the room, he seated himself in the armchair, took a book from his pocket, drew the stand with its candle alongside and began to read.

The man was young—not more than thirty—dark in complexion, smooth-shaven, with brown hair. His face was thin and high-nosed, with a broad forehead and a "firmness" of the chin and jaw which is said by those having it to denote resolution. The eyes were gray and steadfast, not moving except with definitive purpose. They were now for the greater part of the time fixed upon his book, but he occasionally withdrew them and turned them to the body on the table, not, apparently, from any dismal fascination which under such circumstances it might be supposed to exercise upon even a courageous person, nor with a conscious rebellion against the contrary influence which might dominate a timid one. He looked at it as if in his reading he had come upon something recalling him to a sense of his surroundings. Clearly this watcher by the dead was discharging his trust with intelligence and composure, as became him.

After reading for perhaps a half-hour he seemed to come to the end of a chapter and quietly laid away the book. He then rose and taking the reading-stand from the floor carried it into a corner of the room near one of the windows, lifted the candle from it and returned to the empty fireplace before which he had been sitting.

A moment later he walked over to the body on the table, lifted the sheet and turned it back from the head, exposing a mass of dark hair and a thin face-cloth, beneath which the features showed with even sharper definition than before. Shading his eyes by interposing his free hand between them and the candle, he stood looking at his motionless companion with a serious and tranquil regard. Satisfied with his inspection, he pulled the sheet over the face again and returning to the chair, took some matches off the candlestick, put them in the side pocket of his sack-coat and sat down. He then lifted the candle from its socket and looked at it critically, as if calculating how long it would last. It was barely two inches long; in another hour he would be in darkness. He replaced it in the candlestick and blew it out.

II

In a physician's office in Kearny Street three men sat about a table, drinking punch and smoking. It was late in the evening, almost midnight, indeed, and there had been no lack of punch. The gravest of the three, Dr. Helberson, was the host—it was in his rooms they sat. He was about thirty years of age; the others were even younger; all were physicians.

"The superstitious awe with which the living regard the dead," said Dr. Helberson, "is hereditary and incurable. One needs no more be ashamed of it than of the fact that he inherits, for example, an incapacity for mathematics, or a tendency to lie."

The others laughed. "Oughtn't a man to be ashamed to lie?" asked the youngest of the three, who was in fact a medical student not yet graduated.

"My dear Harper, I said nothing about that. The tendency to lie is one thing; lying is another."

"But do you think," said the third man, "that this superstitious feeling, this fear of the dead, reasonless as we know it to be, is universal? I am myself not conscious of it."

"Oh, but it is 'in your system' for all that," replied Helberson; "it needs only the right conditions—what Shakespeare calls the 'confederate season'—to manifest itself in some very disagreeable way that will open your eyes. Physicians and soldiers are of course more nearly free from it than others."

"Physicians and soldiers!—why don't you add hangmen and headsmen? Let us have in all the assassin classes."

"No, my dear Mancher; the juries will not let the public executioners acquire sufficient familiarity with death to be altogether unmoved by it."

Young Harper, who had been helping himself to a fresh cigar at the sideboard, resumed his seat. "What would you consider conditions under which any man of woman born would become insupportably conscious of his share of our common weakness in this regard?" he asked, rather verbosely.

"Well, I should say that if a man were locked up all night with a corpse—alone—in a dark room—of a vacant house—with no bed covers to pull over his head—and lived through it without going altogether mad, he might justly boast himself not of woman born, nor yet, like Macduff, a product of Caesarean section."

"I thought you never would finish piling up conditions," said Harper, "but I know a man who is neither a physician nor a soldier who will accept them all, for any stake you like to name."

"Who is he?"

"His name is Jarette—a stranger here; comes from my town in New York. I have no money to back him, but he will back himself with loads of it."

"How do you know that?"

"He would rather bet than eat. As for fear—I dare say he thinks it some cutaneous disorder, or possibly a particular kind of religious heresy."

"What does he look like?" Helberson was evidently becoming interested.

"Like Mancher, here—might be his twin brother."

"I accept the challenge," said Helberson, promptly.

"Awfully obliged to you for the compliment, I'm sure," drawled Mancher, who was growing sleepy. "Can't I get into this?"

"Not against me," Helberson said. "I don't want *your* money."

"All right," said Mancher; "I'll be the corpse."

The others laughed.
The outcome of this crazy conversation we have seen.

III

In extinguishing his meagre allowance of candle Mr. Jarette's object
was to preserve it against some unforeseen need. He may have
thought, too, or half thought, that the darkness would be no worse
at one time than another, and if the situation became insupportable
it would be better to have a means of relief, or even release. At any
rate it was wise to have a little reserve of light, even if only to enable
him to look at his watch.

No sooner had he blown out the candle and set it on the floor at
his side than he settled himself comfortably in the arm-chair,
leaned back and closed his eyes, hoping and expecting to sleep. In
this he was disappointed; he had never in his life felt less sleepy,
and in a few minutes he gave up the attempt. But what could he do?
He could not go groping about in absolute darkness at the risk of
bruising himself—at the risk, too, of blundering against the table
and rudely disturbing the dead. We all recognize their right to lie
at rest, with immunity from all that is harsh and violent. Jarette
almost succeeded in making himself believe that considerations of
this kind restrained him from risking the collision and fixed him
to the chair.

While thinking of this matter he fancied that he heard a faint
sound in the direction of the table—what kind of sound he could
hardly have explained. He did not turn his head. Why should he—
in the darkness? But he listened—why should he not? And listening he grew giddy and grasped the arms of the chair for support.
There was a strange ringing in his ears; his head seemed bursting;
his chest was oppressed by the constriction of his clothing. He wondered why it was so, and whether these were symptoms of fear.
Then, with a long and strong expiration, his chest appeared to col-
lapse, and with the great gasp with which he refilled his exhausted
lungs the vertigo left him and he knew that so intently had he listened that he had held his breath almost to suffocation. The revelation was vexatious; he arose, pushed away the chair with his foot

and strode to the centre of the room. But one does not stride far in darkness; he began to grope, and finding the wall followed it to an angle, turned, followed it past the two windows and there in another corner came into violent contact with the reading-stand, overturning it. It made a clatter that startled him. He was annoyed. "How the devil could I have forgotten where it was?" he muttered, and groped his way along the third wall to the fireplace. "I must put things to rights," said he, feeling the floor for the candle.

Having recovered that, he lighted it and instantly turned his eyes to the table, where, naturally, nothing had undergone any change. The reading-stand lay unobserved upon the floor: he had forgotten to "put it to rights." He looked all about the room, dispersing the deeper shadows by movements of the candle in his hand, and crossing over to the door tested it by turning and pulling the knob with all his strength. It did not yield and this seemed to afford him a certain satisfaction; indeed, he secured it more firmly by a bolt which he had not before observed. Returning to his chair, he looked at his watch; it was half-past nine. With a start of surprise he held the watch at his ear. It had not stopped. The candle was now visibly shorter. He again extinguished it, placing it on the floor at his side as before.

Mr. Jarette was not at his ease; he was distinctly dissatisfied with his surroundings, and with himself for being so. "What have I to fear?" he thought. "This is ridiculous and disgraceful; I will not be so great a fool." But courage does not come of saying, "I will be courageous," nor of recognizing its appropriateness to the occasion. The more Jarette condemned himself, the more reason he gave himself for condemnation; the greater the number of variations which he played upon the simple theme of the harmlessness of the dead, the more insupportable grew the discord of his emotions. "What!" he cried aloud in the anguish of his spirit, "what! shall I, who have not a shade of superstition in my nature—I, who have no belief in immortality—I, who know (and never more clearly than now) that the after-life is the dream of a desire— shall I lose at once my bet, my honor and my self-respect, perhaps my reason, because certain savage ancestors dwelling in caves and burrows conceived the monstrous notion that the dead walk by night?—that——" Distinctly, unmistakably, Mr. Jarette heard behind him a light, soft sound of footfalls, deliberate, regular, successively nearer!

IV

Just before daybreak the next morning Dr. Helberson and his young friend Harper were driving slowly through the streets of North Beach in the doctor's coupé.

"Have you still the confidence of youth in the courage or stolidity of your friend?" said the elder man. "Do you believe that I have lost this wager?"

"I *know* you have," replied the other, with enfeebling emphasis.

"Well, upon my soul, I hope so."

It was spoken earnestly, almost solemnly. There was a silence for a few moments.

"Harper," the doctor resumed, looking very serious in the shifting half-lights that entered the carriage as they passed the street lamps, "I don't feel altogether comfortable about this business. If your friend had not irritated me by the contemptuous manner in which he treated my doubt of his endurance—a purely physical quality—and by the cool incivility of his suggestion that the corpse be that of a physician, I should not have gone on with it. If anything should happen we are ruined, as I fear we deserve to be."

"What can happen? Even if the matter should be taking a serious turn, of which I am not at all afraid, Mancher has only to 'resurrect' himself and explain matters. With a genuine 'subject' from the dissecting-room, or one of your late patients, it might be different."

Dr. Mancher, then, had been as good as his promise; he was the "corpse."

Dr. Helberson was silent for a long time, as the carriage, at a snail's pace, crept along the same street it had traveled two or three times already. Presently he spoke: "Well, let us hope that Mancher, if he has had to rise from the dead, has been discreet about it. A mistake in that might make matters worse instead of better."

"Yes," said Harper, "Jarette would kill him. But, Doctor"—looking at his watch as the carriage passed a gas lamp—"it is nearly four o'clock at last."

A moment later the two had quitted the vehicle and were walking briskly toward the long-unoccupied house belonging to the doctor in which they had immured Mr. Jarette in accordance with the terms of the mad wager. As they neared it they met a man running. "Can you tell me," he cried, suddenly checking his speed, "where I can find a doctor?"

"What's the matter?" Helberson asked, non-committal.

"Go and see for yourself," said the man, resuming his running.

They hastened on. Arrived at the house, they saw several persons entering in haste and excitement. In some of the dwellings near by and across the way the chamber windows were thrown up, showing a protrusion of heads. All heads were asking questions, none heeding the questions of the others. A few of the windows with closed blinds were illuminated; the inmates of those rooms were dressing to come down. Exactly opposite the door of the house that they sought a street lamp threw a yellow, insufficient light upon the scene, seeming to say that it could disclose a good deal more if it wished. Harper paused at the door and laid a hand upon his companion's arm. "It is all up with us, Doctor," he said in extreme agitation, which contrasted strangely with his free-and-easy words; "the game has gone against us all. Let's not go in there; I'm for lying low."

"I'm a physician," said Dr. Helberson, calmly; "there may be need of one."

They mounted the doorsteps and were about to enter. The door was open; the street lamp opposite lighted the passage into which it opened. It was full of men. Some had ascended the stairs at the farther end, and, denied admittance above, waited for better fortune. All were talking, none listening. Suddenly, on the upper landing there was a great commotion; a man had sprung out of a door and was breaking away from those endeavoring to detain him. Down through the mass of affrighted idlers he came, pushing them aside, flattening them against the wall on one side, or compelling them to cling to the rail on the other, clutching them by the throat, striking them savagely, thrusting them back down the stairs and walking over the fallen. His clothing was in disorder, he was without a hat.

His eyes, wild and restless, had in them something more terrifying than his apparently superhuman strength. His face, smooth-shaven, was bloodless, his hair frost-white.

As the crowd at the foot of the stairs, having more freedom, fell away to let him pass Harper sprang forward. "Jarette! Jarette!" he cried. Dr. Helberson seized Harper by the collar and dragged him back. The man looked into their faces without seeming to see them and sprang through the door, down the steps, into the street, and away. A stout policeman, who had had inferior success in conquering his way down the stairway, followed a moment later and started in pursuit, all the heads in the windows—those of women and children now—screaming in guidance.

The stairway being now partly cleared, most of the crowd having rushed down to the street to observe the flight and pursuit, Dr. Helberson mounted to the landing, followed by Harper. At a door in the upper passage an officer denied them admittance. "We are physicians," said the doctor, and they passed in. The room was full of men, dimly seen, crowded about a table. The newcomers edged their way forward and looked over the shoulders of those in the front rank. Upon the table, the lower limbs covered with a sheet, lay the body of a man, brilliantly illuminated by the beam of a bull's-eye lantern held by a policeman standing at the feet. The others, excepting those near the head—the officer himself—all were in darkness. The face of the body showed yellow, repulsive, horrible! The eyes were partly open and upturned and the jaw fallen; traces of froth defiled the lips, the chin, the cheeks. A tall man, evidently a doctor, bent over the body with his hand thrust under the shirt front. He withdrew it and placed two fingers in the open mouth. "This man has been about six hours dead," said he. "It is a case for the coroner."

He drew a card from his pocket, handed it to the officer and made his way toward the door.

"Clear the room—out, all!" said the officer, sharply, and the body disappeared as if it had been snatched away, as shifting the lantern he flashed its beam of light here and there against the faces of the crowd. The effect was amazing! The men, blinded, confused, almost terrified, made a tumultuous rush for the door, pushing, crowding, and tumbling over one another as they fled, like the hosts of Night before the shafts of Apollo. Upon the struggling, trampling mass the officer poured his light without pity and without cessation. Caught in the current, Helberson and Harper were swept out of the room and cascaded down the stairs into the street.

"Good God, Doctor! did I not tell you that Jarette would kill him?" said Harper, as soon as they were clear of the crowd.

"I believe you did," replied the other, without apparent emotion.

They walked on in silence, block after block. Against the graying east the dwellings of the hill tribes showed in silhouette. The familiar milk wagon was already astir in the streets; the baker's man would soon come upon the scene; the newspaper carrier was abroad in the land.

"It strikes me, youngster," said Helberson, "that you and I have been having too much of the morning air lately. It is unwholesome; we need a change. What do you say to a tour in Europe?"

"When?"

"I'm not particular. I should suppose that four o'clock this afternoon would be early enough."

"I'll meet you at the boat," said Harper.

V

Seven years afterward these two men sat upon a bench in Madison Square, New York, in familiar conversation. Another man, who had been observing them for some time, himself unobserved, approached and, courteously lifting his hat from locks as white as frost, said: "I beg your pardon, gentlemen, but when you have killed a man by coming to life, it is best to change clothes with him, and at the first opportunity make a break for liberty."

Helberson and Harper exchanged significant glances. They were obviously amused. The former then looked the stranger kindly in the eye and replied:

"That has always been my plan. I entirely agree with you as to its advant———"

He stopped suddenly, rose and went white. He stared at the man, open-mouthed; he trembled visibly.

"Ah!" said the stranger, "I see that you are indisposed, Doctor. If you cannot treat yourself Dr. Harper can do something for you, I am sure."

"Who the devil are you?" said Harper, bluntly.

The stranger came nearer and, bending toward them, said in a whisper: "I call myself Jarette sometimes, but I don't mind telling you, for old friendship, that I am Dr. William Mancher."

The revelation brought Harper to his feet. "Mancher!" he cried; and Helberson added: "It is true, by God!"

"Yes," said the stranger, smiling vaguely, "it is true enough, no doubt."

He hesitated and seemed to be trying to recall something, then began humming a popular air. He had apparently forgotten their presence.

"Look here, Mancher," said the elder of the two, "tell us just what occurred that night—to Jarette, you know."

"Oh, yes, about Jarette," said the other. "It's odd I should have neglected to tell you—I tell it so often. You see I knew, by over-hearing him talking to himself, that he was pretty badly frightened. So I couldn't resist the temptation to come to life and have a bit of fun out of him—I couldn't really. That was all right, though certainly I did not think he would take it so seriously; I did not, truly. And afterward—well, it was a tough job changing places with him, and then—damn you! you didn't let me out!"

Nothing could exceed the ferocity with which these last words were delivered. Both men stepped back in alarm.

"We?—why—why," Helberson stammered, losing his self-possession utterly, "we had nothing to do with it."

"Didn't I say you were Drs. Hellborn and Sharper?" inquired the man, laughing.

"My name is Helberson, yes; and this gentleman is Mr. Harper," replied the former, reassured by the laugh. "But we are not physicians now; we are—well, hang it, old man, we are gamblers."

And that was the truth.

"A very good profession—very good, indeed; and, by the way, I hope Sharper here paid over Jarette's money like an honest stakeholder. A very good and honorable profession," he repeated, thoughtfully, moving carelessly away; "but I stick to the old one. I am High Supreme Medical Officer of the Bloomingdale Asylum; it is my duty to cure the superintendent."

The Man and the Snake

*It is of veritabyll report, and attested of so many that there be
nowe of wyse and learned none to gaynsaye it, that ye serpente hys
eye hath a magnetick propertie that whosoe falleth into its svasion
is drawn forwards in despyte of his wille, and perisheth miserabyll
by ye creature hys byte.*

Stretched at ease upon a sofa, in gown and slippers, Harker Brayton
smiled as he read the foregoing sentence in old Morryster's *Marvells
of Science*. "The only marvel in the matter," he said to himself, "is
that the wise and learned in Morryster's day should have believed
such nonsense as is rejected by most of even the ignorant in ours."

A train of reflection followed—for Brayton was a man of
thought—and he unconsciously lowered his book without altering
the direction of his eyes. As soon as the volume had gone below the
line of sight, something in an obscure corner of the room recalled
his attention to his surroundings. What he saw, in the shadow
under his bed, was two small points of light, apparently about an
inch apart. They might have been reflections of the gas jet above
him, in metal nail heads; he gave them but little thought and
resumed his reading. A moment later something—some impulse
which it did not occur to him to analyze—impelled him to lower
the book again and seek for what he saw before. The points of light
were still there. They seemed to have become brighter than before,
shining with a greenish lustre that he had not at first observed. He
thought, too, that they might have moved a trifle—were somewhat

nearer. They were still too much in shadow, however, to reveal their nature and origin to an indolent attention, and again he resumed his reading. Suddenly something in the text suggested a thought that made him start and drop the book for the third time to the side of the sofa, whence, escaping from his hand, it fell sprawling to the floor, back upward. Brayton, half-risen, was staring intently into the obscurity beneath the bed, where the points of light shone with, it seemed to him, an added fire. His attention was now fully aroused, his gaze eager and imperative. It disclosed, almost directly under the foot-rail of the bed, the coils of a large serpent—the points of light were its eyes! Its horrible head, thrust flatly forth from the innermost coil and resting upon the outermost, was directed straight toward him, the definition of the wide, brutal jaw and the idiot-like forehead serving to show the direction of its malevolent gaze. The eyes were no longer merely luminous points; they looked into his own with a meaning, a malign significance.

II

A snake in a bedroom of a modern city dwelling of the better sort is, happily, not so common a phenomenon as to make explanation altogether needless. Harker Brayton, a bachelor of thirty-five, a scholar, idler and something of an athlete, rich, popular and of sound health, had returned to San Francisco from all manner of remote and unfamiliar countries. His tastes, always a trifle luxurious, had taken on an added exuberance from long privation; and the resources of even the Castle Hotel being inadequate to their perfect gratification, he had gladly accepted the hospitality of his friend, Dr. Druring, the distinguished scientist. Dr. Druring's house, a large, old-fashioned one in what is now an obscure quarter of the city, had an outer and visible aspect of proud reserve. It plainly would not associate with the contiguous elements of its altered environment, and appeared to have developed some of the eccentricities which come of isolation. One of these was a "wing," conspicuously irrelevant in point of architecture, and no less rebellious in matter of purpose; for it was a combination of laboratory, menagerie and museum. It was here that the doctor indulged the scientific side of his nature in the study of such forms of animal life as engaged his interest and comforted his taste—which, it must be confessed, ran rather to the lower types. For one of the higher nimbly and sweetly to recommend itself unto his gentle senses it had at least to retain certain rudimentary characteristics allying it to such "dragons of the prime" as toads and snakes. His scientific sympathies were distinctly reptilian; he loved nature's vulgarians and described himself as the Zola of zoölogy. His wife and daughters not having the advantage to share his enlightened curiosity regarding the works and ways of our ill-starred fellow-creatures, were with needless austerity excluded from what he called the Snakery and doomed to companionship with their own kind, though to soften the rigors of their lot he had permitted them out of his great wealth to outdo the reptiles in the gorgeousness of their surroundings and to shine with a superior splendor.

Architecturally and in point of "furnishing" the Snakery had a severe simplicity befitting the humble circumstances of its occupants, many of whom, indeed, could not safely have been intrusted with the liberty that is necessary to the full enjoyment of luxury, for they have the troublesome peculiarity of being alive. In their own apartments, however, they were under as little personal restraint as was compatible with their protection from the baneful habit of swallowing one another; and, as Brayton had thoughtfully been apprised, it was more than a tradition that some of them had at divers times been found in parts of the premises where it would have embarrassed them to explain their presence. Despite the Snakery and its uncanny associations—to which, indeed, he gave little attention—Brayton found life at the Druring mansion very much to his mind.

III

Beyond a smart shock of surprise and a shudder of mere loathing Mr. Brayton was not greatly affected. His first thought was to ring the call bell and bring a servant; but although the bell cord dangled within easy reach he made no movement toward it; it had occurred to his mind that the act might subject him to the suspicion of fear, which he certainly did not feel. He was more keenly conscious of the incongruous nature of the situation than affected by its perils; it was revolting, but absurd.

The reptile was of a species with which Brayton was unfamiliar. Its length he could only conjecture; the body at the largest visible part seemed about as thick as his forearm. In what way was it dangerous, if in any way? Was it venomous? Was it a constrictor? His knowledge of nature's danger signals did not enable him to say; he had never deciphered the code.

If not dangerous the creature was at least offensive. It was *de trop*—"matter out of place"—an impertinence. The gem was unworthy of the setting. Even the barbarous taste of our time and country, which had loaded the walls of the room with pictures, the floor with furniture and the furniture with bric-a-brac, had not quite fitted the place for this bit of the savage life of the jungle. Besides—insupportable thought!—the exhalations of its breath mingled with the atmosphere which he himself was breathing.

These thoughts shaped themselves with greater or less definition in Brayton's mind and begot action. The process is what we call consideration and decision. It is thus that we are wise and unwise. It is thus that the withered leaf in an autumn breeze shows greater or less intelligence than its fellows, falling upon the land or upon the lake. The secret of human action is an open one: something contracts our muscles. Does it matter if we give to the preparatory molecular changes the name of will?

Brayton rose to his feet and prepared to back softly away from the snake, without disturbing it if possible, and through the door. Men retire so from the presence of the great, for greatness is power and power is a menace. He knew that he could walk backward without error. Should the monster follow, the taste which had plastered the walls with paintings had consistently supplied a rack of murderous Oriental weapons from which he could snatch one to suit the occasion. In the mean time the snake's eyes burned with a more pitiless malevolence than before.

Brayton lifted his right foot free of the floor to step backward. That moment he felt a strong aversion to doing so.

"I am accounted brave," he thought; "is bravery, then, no more

than pride? Because there are none to witness the shame shall I
retreat?"

He was steadying himself with his right hand upon the back of
a chair, his foot suspended.

"Nonsense!" he said aloud; "I am not so great a coward as to fear
to seem to myself afraid."

He lifted the foot a little higher by slightly bending the knee and
thrust it sharply to the floor—an inch in front of the other! He
could not think how that occurred. A trial with the left foot had
the same result; it was again in advance of the right. The hand upon
the chair back was grasping it; the arm was straight, reaching somewhat backward. One might have said that he was reluctant to lose
his hold. The snake's malignant head was still thrust forth from the
inner coil as before, the neck level. It had not moved, but its eyes
were now electric sparks, radiating an infinity of luminous needles.

The man had an ashy pallor. Again he took a step forward, and
another, partly dragging the chair, which when finally released fell
upon the floor with a crash. The man groaned; the snake made neither sound nor motion, but its eyes were two dazzling suns. The reptile itself was wholly concealed by them. They gave off enlarging
rings of rich and vivid colors, which at their greatest expansion successively vanished like soap-bubbles; they seemed to approach his
very face, and anon were an immeasurable distance away. He heard,
somewhere, the continuous throbbing of a great drum, with desultory bursts of far music, inconceivably sweet, like the tones of an æolian
harp. He knew it for the sunrise melody of Memnon's statue, and
thought he stood in the Nileside reeds hearing with exalted sense
that immortal anthem through the silence of the centuries.

The music ceased; rather, it became by insensible degrees the distant roll of a retreating thunder-storm. A landscape, glittering with
sun and rain, stretched before him, arched with a vivid rainbow
framing in its giant curve a hundred visible cities. In the middle
distance a vast serpent, wearing a crown, reared its head out of its
voluminous convolutions and looked at him with his dead mother's eyes. Suddenly this enchanting landscape seemed to rise swiftly
upward like the drop scene at a theatre, and vanished in a blank.
Something struck him a hard blow upon the face and breast. He

had fallen to the floor; the blood ran from his broken nose and his bruised lips. For a time he was dazed and stunned, and lay with closed eyes, his face against the floor. In a few moments he had recovered, and then knew that this fall, by withdrawing his eyes, had broken the spell that held him. He felt that now, by keeping his gaze averted, he would be able to retreat. But the thought of the serpent within a few feet of his head, yet unseen—perhaps in the very act of springing upon him and throwing its coils about his throat—was too horrible! He lifted his head, stared again into those baleful eyes and was again in bondage.

The snake had not moved and appeared somewhat to have lost its power upon the imagination; the gorgeous illusions of a few moments before were not repeated. Beneath that flat and brainless brow its black, beady eyes simply glittered as at first with an expression unspeakably malignant. It was as if the creature, assured of its triumph, had determined to practise no more alluring wiles.

Now ensued a fearful scene. The man, prone upon the floor, within a yard of his enemy, raised the upper part of his body upon his elbows, his head thrown back, his legs extended to their full length. His face was white between its stains of blood; his eyes were strained open to their uttermost expansion. There was froth upon his lips; it dropped off in flakes. Strong convulsions ran through his body, making almost serpentile undulations. He bent himself at the waist, shifting his legs from side to side. And every movement left him a little nearer to the snake. He thrust his hands forward to brace himself back, yet constantly advanced upon his elbows.

IV

Dr. Druring and his wife sat in the library. The scientist was in rare good humor.

"I have just obtained by exchange with another collector," he said, "a splendid specimen of the *ophiophagus*."

"And what may that be?" the lady inquired with a somewhat languid interest.

"Why, bless my soul, what profound ignorance! My dear, a man who ascertains after marriage that his wife does not know Greek is entitled to a divorce. The *ophiophagus* is a snake that eats other snakes."

"I hope it will eat all yours," she said, absently shifting the lamp. "But how does it get the other snakes? By charming them, I suppose."

"That is just like you, dear," said the doctor, with an affectation of petulance. "You know how irritating to me is any allusion to that vulgar superstition about a snake's power of fascination."

The conversation was interrupted by a mighty cry, which rang through the silent house like the voice of a demon shouting in a tomb! Again and yet again it sounded, with terrible distinctness. They sprang to their feet, the man confused, the lady pale and speechless with fright. Almost before the echoes of the last cry had died away the doctor was out of the room, springing up the stairs two steps at a time. In the corridor in front of Brayton's chamber he met some servants who had come from the upper floor. Together they rushed at the door without knocking. It was unfastened and gave way. Brayton lay upon his stomach on the floor, dead. His head and arms were partly concealed under the foot rail of the bed. They pulled the body away, turning it upon the back. The face was daubed with blood and froth, the eyes were wide open, staring—a dreadful sight!

"Died in a fit," said the scientist, bending his knee and placing his hand upon the heart. While in that position, he chanced to look under the bed. "Good God!" he added, "how did this thing get in here?"

He reached under the bed, pulled out the snake and flung it, still coiled, to the center of the room, whence with a harsh, shuffling sound it slid across the polished floor till stopped by the wall, where it lay without motion. It was a stuffed snake; its eyes were two shoe buttons.

Chickamauga

One sunny autumn afternoon a child strayed away from its rude home in a small field and entered a forest unobserved. It was happy in a new sense of freedom from control, happy in the opportunity of exploration and adventure; for this child's spirit, in bodies of its ancestors, had for thousands of years been trained to memorable feats of discovery and conquest—victories in battles whose critical moments were centuries, whose victors' camps were cities of hewn stone. From the cradle of its race it had conquered its way through two continents and passing a great sea had penetrated a third, there to be born to war and dominion as a heritage.

The child was a boy aged about six years, the son of a poor planter. In his younger manhood the father had been a soldier, had fought against naked savages and followed the flag of his country into the capital of a civilized race to the far South. In the peaceful life of a planter the warrior-fire survived; once kindled, it is never extinguished. The man loved military books and pictures and the boy had understood enough to make himself a wooden sword, though even the eye of his father would hardly have known it for what it was. This weapon he now bore bravely, as became the son of an heroic race, and pausing now and again in the sunny space of the forest assumed, with some exaggeration, the postures of aggression and defense that he had been taught by the engraver's art. Made reckless by the ease with which he overcame invisible foes attempting to stay his advance, he committed the common enough military error of pushing the pursuit to a dangerous extreme, until he found himself upon the margin of a wide but shallow brook, whose rapid waters barred his direct advance against the flying foe that had crossed with illogical ease. But the intrepid victor was not to be baffled; the spirit of the race which had passed the great sea burned unconquerable in that small breast and would not be denied. Finding a place where some bowlders in the bed of the stream lay but a step or a leap apart, he made his way across and fell again upon the rear-guard of his imaginary foe, putting all to the sword.

Now that the battle had been won, prudence required that he withdraw to his base of operations. Alas; like many a mightier conqueror, and like one, the mightiest, he could not

curb the lust for war,
Nor learn that tempted Fate will leave the loftiest star.

Advancing from the bank of the creek he suddenly found himself confronted with a new and more formidable enemy: in the path that he was following, sat, bolt upright, with ears erect and paws suspended before it, a rabbit! With a startled cry the child turned and fled, he knew not in what direction, calling with inarticulate cries for his mother, weeping, stumbling, his tender skin cruelly torn by brambles, his little heart beating hard with terror—breathless, blind with tears—lost in the forest! Then, for more than an hour, he wandered with erring feet through the tangled undergrowth, till at last, overcome by fatigue, he lay down in a narrow space between two rocks, within a few yards of the stream and still grasping his toy sword, no longer a weapon but a companion, sobbed himself to sleep. The wood birds sang merrily above his head; the squirrels, whisking their bravery of tail, ran barking from tree to tree, unconscious of the pity of it, and somewhere far away was a strange, muffled thunder, as if the partridges were drumming in celebration of nature's victory over the son of her immemorial enslavers. And back at the little plantation, where white men and black were hastily searching the fields and hedges in alarm, a mother's heart was breaking for her missing child.

Hours passed, and then the little sleeper rose to his feet. The chill of the evening was in his limbs, the fear of the gloom in his heart. But he had rested, and he no longer wept. With some blind instinct which impelled to action he struggled through the undergrowth about him and came to a more open ground—on his right the brook, to the left a gentle acclivity studded with infrequent trees; over all, the gathering gloom of twilight. A thin, ghostly mist rose along the water. It frightened and repelled him; instead of recrossing, in the direction whence he had come, he turned his back upon it, and went forward toward the dark inclosing wood. Suddenly he saw before him a strange moving object which he took to be some large animal—a dog, a pig—he could not name it; perhaps it was a bear. He had seen pictures of bears, but knew of nothing to their discredit and had vaguely wished to meet one. But something in form or movement of this object—something in the awkwarkness of its approach—told him that it was not a bear, and curiosity was stayed by fear. He stood still and as it came slowly on gained courage every moment, for he saw that at least it had not the long, menacing ears of the rabbit. Possibly his impressionable mind was half conscious of something familiar in its shambling, awkward gait. Before it had approached near enough to resolve his doubts he saw that it was followed by another and another. To right and to left were many more, the whole open space about him was alive with them—all moving toward the brook.

They were men. They crept upon their hands and knees. They used their hands only, dragging their legs. They used their knees only, their arms hanging idle at their sides. They strove to rise to their feet, but fell prone in the attempt. They did nothing naturally, and nothing alike, save only to advance foot by foot in the same direction. Singly, in pairs and in little groups, they came on through the gloom, some halting now and again while others crept slowly past them, then resuming their movement. They came by dozens and by hundreds; as far on either hand as one could see in the deepening gloom they extended and the black wood behind them appeared to be inexhaustible. The very ground seemed in motion toward the creek. Occasionally one who had paused did not again go on, but lay motionless. He was dead. Some, pausing, made strange gestures with their hands, erected their arms and lowered them again, clasped their heads; spread their palms upward, as men are sometimes seen to do in public prayer.

Not all of this did the child note; it is what would have been noted by an elder observer; he saw little but that these were men, yet crept like babes. Being men, they were not terrible, though unfamiliarly clad. He moved among them freely, going from one to another and peering into their faces with childish curiosity. All their faces were singularly white and many were streaked and gouted with red. Something in this—something too, perhaps, in their grotesque attitudes and movements—reminded him of the painted clown whom he had seen last summer in the circus, and he laughed as he watched them. But on and ever on they crept, these maimed and bleeding men, as heedless as he of the dramatic contrast between his laughter and their own ghastly gravity. To him it was a merry spectacle. He had seen his father's negroes creep upon their hands and knees for his amusement—had ridden them so, "making believe" they were his horses. He now approached one of these crawling figures from behind and with an agile movement mounted it astride. The man sank upon his breast, recovered, flung the small boy fiercely to the ground as an unbroken colt might have done, then turned upon him a face that lacked a lower jaw—from the upper teeth to the throat was a great red gap fringed with hanging shreds of flesh and splinters of bone. The unnatural prominence of nose, the absence of chin, the fierce eyes, gave this man the appearance of a great bird of prey crimsoned in throat and breast by the blood of its quarry. The man rose to his knees, the child to his feet. The man shook his fist at the child; the child, terrified at last, ran to a tree near by, got upon the farther side of it and took a more serious view of the situation. And so the clumsy multitude dragged itself slowly and painfully along in hideous pantomime—moved forward down the slope like a swarm of great black beetles, with never a sound of going—in silence profound, absolute.

Instead of darkening, the haunted landscape began to brighten. Through the belt of trees beyond the brook shone a strange red light, the trunks and branches of the trees making a black lacework against it. It struck the creeping figures and gave them monstrous shadows, which caricatured their movements on the lit grass. It fell upon their faces, touching their whiteness with a ruddy tinge, accentuating the stains with which so many of them were freaked and maculated. It sparkled on buttons and bits of metal in their clothing. Instinctively the child turned toward the growing splendor and moved down the slope with his horrible companions; in a few moments had passed the foremost of the throng—not much of a feat, considering his advantages. He placed himself in the lead, his wooden sword still in hand, and solemnly directed the march, conforming his pace to theirs and occasionally turning as if to see that his forces did not straggle. Surely such a leader never before had such a following.

Scattered about upon the ground now slowly narrowing by the encroachment of this awful march to water, were certain articles to which, in the leader's mind, were coupled no significant associations: an occasional blanket, tightly rolled lengthwise, doubled and the ends bound together with a string; a heavy knapsack here, and there a broken rifle—such things, in short, as are found in the rear of retreating troops, the "spoor" of men flying from their hunters. Everywhere near the creek, which here had a margin of lowland, the earth was trodden into mud by the feet of men and horses. An observer of better experience in the use of his eyes would have noticed that these footprints pointed in both directions; the ground had been twice passed over—in advance and in retreat. A few hours before, these desperate, stricken men, with their more fortunate and now distant comrades, had penetrated the forest in thousands. Their successive battalions, breaking into swarms and re-forming in lines, had passed the child on every side—had almost trodden on him as he slept. The rustle and murmur of their march had not awakened him. Almost within a stone's throw of where he lay they had fought a battle; but all unheard by him were the roar of the musketry, the shock of the cannon, "the thunder of the captains and the shouting." He had slept through it all, grasping his little wooden sword with perhaps a tighter clutch in unconscious sympathy with his martial environment, but as heedless of the grandeur of the struggle as the dead who had died to make the glory.

The fire beyond the belt of woods on the farther side of the creek, reflected to earth from the canopy of its own smoke, was now suffusing the whole landscape. It transformed the sinuous line of mist to the vapor of gold. The water gleamed with dashes of red, and red, too, were many of the stones protruding above the surface. But that was blood; the less desperately wounded had stained them in crossing. On them, too, the child now crossed with eager steps; he was going to the fire. As he stood upon the farther bank he turned about to look at the companions of his march. The advance was arriving at the creek. The stronger had already drawn themselves to the brink and plunged their faces into the flood. Three or four who lay without motion appeared to have no heads. At this the child's eyes expanded with wonder; even his hospitable understanding could not accept a phenomenon implying such vitality as that. After slaking their thirst these men had not had the strength to back away from the water, nor to keep their heads above it. They were drowned. In rear of these, the open spaces of the forest showed the leader as many formless figures of his grim command as at first; but not nearly so many were in motion. He waved his cap for their encouragement and smilingly pointed with his weapon in the direction of the guiding light— a pillar of fire to this strange exodus.

Confident of the fidelity of his forces, he now entered the belt of woods, passed through it easily in the red illumination, climbed a fence, ran across a field, turning now and again to coquet with his responsive shadow, and so approached the blazing ruin of a dwelling. Desolation everywhere! In all the wide glare not a living thing was visible. He cared nothing for that; the spectacle pleased, and he danced with glee in imitation of the wavering flames. He ran about, collecting fuel, but every object that he found was too heavy for him to cast in from the distance to which the heat limited his approach. In despair he flung in his sword—a surrender to the superior forces of nature. His military career was at an end.

Shifting his position, his eyes fell upon some outbuildings which had an oddly familiar appearance, as if he had dreamed of them. He stood considering them with wonder, when suddenly the entire plantation, with its inclosing forest, seemed to turn as if upon a pivot. His little world swung half around; the points of the compass were reversed. He recognized the blazing building as his own home!

For a moment he stood stupefied by the power of the revelation, then ran with stumbling feet, making a half-circuit of the ruin.

There, conspicuous in the light of the conflagration, lay the dead
body of a woman—the white face turned upward, the hands
thrown out and clutched full of grass, the clothing deranged, the
long dark hair in tangles and full of clotted blood. The greater part
of the forehead was torn away, and from the jagged hole the brain
protruded, overflowing the temple, a frothy mass of gray, crowned
with clusters of crimson bubbles—the work of a shell.

The child moved his little hands, making wild, uncertain gestures. He uttered a series of inarticulate and indescribable cries—
something between the chattering of an ape and the gobbling of a
turkey—a startling, soulless, unholy sound, the language of a devil.
The child was a deaf mute.

Then he stood motionless, with quivering lips, looking down
upon the wreck.

An Occurrence at Owl Creek Bridge

I

A man stood upon a railroad bridge in northern Alabama, looking down into the swift water twenty feet below. The man's hands were behind his back, the wrists bound with a cord. A rope closely encircled his neck. It was attached to a stout cross-timber above his head and the slack fell to the level of his knees. Some loose boards laid upon the sleepers supporting the metals of the railway supplied a footing for him and his executioners—two private soldiers of the Federal army, directed by a sergeant who in civil life may have been a deputy sheriff. At a short remove upon the same temporary platform was an officer in the uniform of his rank, armed. He was a captain. A sentinel at each end of the bridge stood with his rifle in the position known as "support," that is to say, vertical in front of the left shoulder, the hammer resting on the forearm thrown straight across the chest—a formal and unnatural position, enforcing an erect carriage of the body. It did not appear to be the duty of these two men to know what was occurring at the centre of the bridge; they merely blockaded the two ends of the foot planking that traversed it.

Beyond one of the sentinels nobody was in sight; the railroad ran straight away into a forest for a hundred yards, then, curving, was lost to view. Doubtless there was an outpost farther along. The other bank of the stream was open ground—a gentle acclivity topped with a stockade of vertical tree trunks, loopholed for rifles, with a single embrasure through which protruded the muzzle of a brass cannon commanding the bridge. Midway of the slope between bridge and fort were the spectators—a single company of infantry in line, at "parade rest," the butts of the rifles on the ground, the barrels inclining slightly backward against the right shoulder, the hands crossed upon the stock. A lieutenant stood at the right of the line, the point of his sword upon the ground, his left hand resting upon his right. Excepting the group of four at the centre of the bridge, not a man moved. The company faced the bridge, staring stonily, motionless. The sentinels, facing the banks of the stream, might have been statues to adorn the bridge. The captain stood with folded arms, silent, observing the work of his subordinates, but making no sign. Death is a dignitary who when he comes announced is to be received with formal manifestations of respect, even by those most familiar with him. In the code of military etiquette silence and fixity are forms of deference.

The man who was engaged in being hanged was apparently about thirty-five years of age. He was a civilian, if one might judge from his habit, which was that of a planter. His features were good—a straight nose, firm mouth, broad forehead, from which his long, dark hair was combed straight back, falling behind his ears to the collar of his well-fitting frock-coat. He wore a mustache and pointed beard, but no whiskers; his eyes were large and dark gray, and had a kindly expression which one would hardly have expected in one whose neck was in the hemp. Evidently this was no vulgar assassin. The liberal military code makes provision for hanging many kinds of persons, and gentlemen are not excluded.

The preparations being complete, the two private soldiers stepped aside and each drew away the plank upon which he had been standing. The sergeant turned to the captain, saluted and placed himself immediately behind that officer, who in turn moved apart one pace. These movements left the condemned man and the sergeant standing on the two ends of the same plank, which spanned three of the cross-ties of the bridge. The end upon which the civilian stood almost, but not quite, reached a fourth. This plank had been held in place by the weight of the captain; it was now held by that of the sergeant. At a signal from the former the latter would step aside, the plank would tilt and the condemned man go down between two ties. The arrangement commended itself to his judgment as simple and effective. His face had not been covered nor his eyes bandaged. He looked a moment at his "unsteadfast footing," then let his gaze wander to the swirling water of the stream racing madly beneath his feet. A piece of dancing driftwood caught his attention and his eyes followed it down the current. How slowly it appeared to move! What a sluggish stream!

He closed his eyes in order to fix his last thoughts upon his wife and children. The water, touched to gold by the early sun, the brooding mists under the banks at some distance down the stream, the fort, the soldiers, the piece of drift—all had distracted him. And now he became conscious of a new disturbance. Striking through the thought of his dear ones was a sound which he could neither ignore nor understand, a sharp, distinct, metallic percussion like the stroke of a blacksmith's hammer upon the anvil; it had the same ringing quality. He wondered what it was, and whether immeasurably distant or near by—it seemed both. Its recurrence was regular, but as slow as the tolling of a death knell. He awaited each stroke with impatience and—he knew not why—apprehension. The intervals of silence grew progressively longer; the delays became maddening. With their greater infrequency the sounds increased in strength and sharpness. They hurt his ear like the thrust of a knife; he feared he would shriek. What he heard was the ticking of his watch.

He unclosed his eyes and saw again the water below him. "If I could free my hands," he thought, "I might throw off the noose and spring into the stream. By diving I could evade the bullets and, swimming vigorously, reach the bank, take to the woods and get away home. My home, thank God, is as yet outside their lines; my wife and little ones are still beyond the invader's farthest advance."

As these thoughts, which have here to be set down in words, were flashed into the doomed man's brain rather than evolved from it the captain nodded to the sergeant. The sergeant stepped aside.

II

Peyton Farquhar was a well-to-do planter, of an old and highly respected Alabama family. Being a slave owner and like other slave owners a politician he was naturally an original secessionist and ardently devoted to the Southern cause. Circumstances of an imperious nature, which it is unnecessary to relate here, had prevented him from taking service with the gallant army that had fought the disastrous campaigns ending with the fall of Corinth, and he chafed under the inglorious restraint, longing for the release of his energies, the larger life of the soldier, the opportunity for distinction. That opportunity, he felt, would come, as it comes to all in war time. Meanwhile he did what he could. No service was too humble for him to perform in aid of the South, no adventure too perilous for him to undertake if consistent with the character of a civilian who was at heart a soldier, and who in good faith and without too much qualification assented to at least a part of the frankly villainous dictum that all is fair in love and war.

One evening while Farquhar and his wife were sitting on a rustic bench near the entrance to his grounds, a gray-clad soldier rode up to the gate and asked for a drink of water. Mrs. Farquhar was only too happy to serve him with her own white hands. While she was fetching the water her husband approached the dusty horseman and inquired eagerly for news from the front.

"The Yanks are repairing the railroads," said the man, "and are getting ready for another advance. They have reached the Owl Creek bridge, put it in order and built a stockade on the north bank. The commandant has issued an order, which is posted everywhere, declaring that any civilian caught interfering with the railroad, its bridges, tunnels or trains will be summarily hanged. I saw the order."

"How far is it to the Owl Creek bridge?" Farquhar asked.

"About thirty miles."

"Is there no force on this side the creek?"

"Only a picket post half a mile out, on the railroad, and a single sentinel at this end of the bridge."

"Suppose a man—a civilian and student of hanging—should elude the picket post and perhaps get the better of the sentinel," said Farquhar, smiling, "what could he accomplish?"

The soldier reflected. "I was there a month ago," he replied. "I observed that the flood of last winter had lodged a great quantity of driftwood against the wooden pier at this end of the bridge. It is now dry and would burn like tow."

The lady had now brought the water, which the soldier drank. He thanked her ceremoniously, bowed to her husband and rode away. An hour later, after nightfall, he repassed the plantation, going northward in the direction from which he had come. He was a Federal Scout.

III

As Peyton Farquhar fell straight downward through the bridge he lost consciousness and was as one already dead. From this state he was awakened—ages later, it seemed to him—by the pain of a sharp pressure upon his throat, followed by a sense of suffocation. Keen, poignant agonies seemed to shoot from his neck downward through every fibre of his body and limbs. These pains appeared to flash along well-defined lines of ramification and to beat with an inconceivably rapid periodicity. They seemed like streams of pulsating fire heating him to an intolerable temperature. As to his head, he was conscious of nothing but a feeling of fullness—of congestion. These sensations were unaccompanied by thought. The intellectual part of his nature was already effaced; he had power only to feel, and feeling was torment. He was conscious of motion. Encompassed in a luminous cloud, of which he was now merely the fiery heart, without material substance, he swung through unthinkable arcs of oscillation, like a vast pendulum. Then all at once, with terrible suddenness, the light about him shot upward with the noise of a loud plash; a frightful roaring was in his ears, and all was cold and dark. The power of thought was restored; he knew that the rope had broken and he had fallen into the stream. There was no additional strangulation; the noose about his neck was already suffocating him and kept the water from his lungs. To die of hanging at the bottom of a river!—the idea seemed to him ludicrous. He opened his eyes in the darkness and saw above him a gleam of light, but how distant, how inaccessible! He was still sinking, for the light became fainter and fainter until it was a mere glimmer. Then it began to grow and brighten, and he knew that he was rising toward the surface—knew it with reluctance, for he was now very comfortable. "To be hanged and drowned," he thought, "that is not so bad; but I do not wish to be shot. No; I will not be shot; that is not fair."

He was not conscious of an effort, but a sharp pain in his wrist apprised him that he was trying to free his hands. He gave the struggle his attention, as an idler might observe the feat of a juggler, without interest in the outcome. What splendid effort!—what magnificent, what superhuman strength! Ah, that was a fine endeavor! Bravo! The cord fell away; his arms parted and floated upward, the hands dimly seen on each side in the growing light. He watched them with a new interest as first one and then the other pounced upon the noose at his neck. They tore it away and thrust it fiercely aside, its undulations resembling those of a water-snake. "Put it back, put it back!" He thought he shouted these words to his hands, for the undoing of the noose had been succeeded by the direst pang that he had yet experienced. His neck ached horribly; his brain was on fire; his heart, which had been fluttering faintly, gave a great leap, trying to force itself out at his mouth. His whole body was racked and wrenched with an insupportable anguish! But his disobedient hands gave no heed to the command. They beat the water vigorously with quick, downward strokes, forcing him to the surface. He felt his head emerge; his eyes were blinded by the sunlight; his chest expanded convulsively, and with a supreme and crowning agony his lungs engulfed a great draught of air, which instantly he expelled in a shriek!

He was now in full possession of his physical senses. They were, indeed, preternaturally keen and alert. Something in the awful disturbance of his organic system had so exalted and refined them that they made record of things never before perceived. He felt the ripples upon his face and heard their separate sounds as they struck. He looked at the forest on the bank of the stream, saw the individual trees, the leaves and the veining of each leaf—saw the very insects upon them: the locusts, the brilliant-bodied flies, the gray spiders stretching their webs from twig to twig. He noted the prismatic colors in all the dewdrops upon a million blades of grass. The humming of the gnats that danced above the eddies of the stream, the beating of the dragon-flies' wings, the strokes of the water-spiders' legs, like oars which had lifted their boat—all these made audible music. A fish slid along beneath his eyes and he heard the rush of its body parting the water.

He had come to the surface facing down the stream; in a moment the visible world seemed to wheel slowly round, himself the pivotal point, and he saw the bridge, the fort, the soldiers upon the bridge, the captain, the sergeant, the two privates, his executioners. They were in silhouette against the blue sky. They shouted and gesticu- lated, pointing at him. The captain had drawn his pistol, but did not fire; the others were unarmed. Their movements were grotesque and horrible, their forms gigantic.

Suddenly he heard a sharp report and something struck the water smartly within a few inches of his head, spattering his face with spray. He heard a second report, and saw one of the sentinels with his rifle at his shoulder, a light cloud of blue smoke rising from the muzzle. The man in the water saw the eye of the man on the bridge gazing into his own through the sights of the rifle. He observed that it was a gray eye and remembered having read that gray eyes were keenest, and that all famous marksmen had them. Nevertheless, this one had missed.

A counter-swirl had caught Farquhar and turned him half round; he was again looking into the forest on the bank opposite the fort. The sound of a clear, high voice in a monotonous singsong now rang out behind him and came across the water with a distinct- ness that pierced and subdued all other sounds, even the beating of the ripples in his ears. Although no soldier, he had frequented camps enough to know the dread significance of that deliberate, drawling, aspirated chant; the lieutenant on shore was taking a part in the morning's work. How coldly and pitilessly—with what an even, calm intonation, presaging, and enforcing tranquility in the men—with what accurately measured intervals fell those cruel words:

"Attention, company!...Shoulder arms!...Ready! Aim!...Fire!"

Farquhar dived—dived as deeply as he could. The water roared in his ears like the voice of Niagara, yet he heard the dulled thunder of the volley and, rising again toward the surface, met shining bits of metal, singularly flattened, oscillating slowly downward. Some of them touched him on the face and hands, then fell away, continuing their descent. One lodged between his collar and neck; it was uncomfortably warm and he snatched it out.

As he rose to the surface, gasping for breath, he saw that he had been a long time under water; he was perceptibly farther down stream—nearer to safety. The soldiers had almost finished reloading; the metal ramrods flashed all at once in the sunshine as they were drawn from the barrels, turned in the air, and thrust into their sockets. The two sentinels fired again, independently and ineffectually.

The hunted man saw all this over his shoulder; he was now swimming vigorously with the current. His brain was as energetic as his arms and legs; he thought with the rapidity of lightning.

"The officer," he reasoned, "will not make that martinet's error a second time. It is as easy to dodge a volley as a single shot. He has probably already given the command to fire at will. God help me, I cannot dodge them all!"

An appalling plash within two yards of him was followed by a loud, rushing sound, *diminuendo,* which seemed to travel back through the air to the fort and died in an explosion which stirred the very river to its deeps! A rising sheet of water curved over him, fell down upon him, blinded him, strangled him! The cannon had taken a hand in the game. As he shook his head free from the commotion of the smitten water he heard the deflected shot humming through the air ahead, and in an instant it was cracking and and smashing the branches in the forest beyond.

"They will not do that again," he thought; "the next time they will use a charge of grape. I must keep my eye upon the gun; the smoke will apprise me—the report arrives too late; it lags behind the missile. That is a good gun."

Suddenly he felt himself whirled round and round—spinning like a top. The water, the banks, the forests, the now distant bridge, fort and men—all were commingled and blurred. Objects were represented by their colors only; circular horizontal streaks of color—that was all he saw. He had been caught in a vortex and was being whirled on with a velocity of advance and gyration that made him giddy and sick. In a few moments he was flung upon the gravel at the foot of the left bank of the stream—the southern bank—and behind a projecting point which concealed him from his enemies. The sudden arrest of his motion, the abrasion of one of his hands on the gravel, restored him, and he wept with delight. He dug his fingers into the sand, threw it over himself in handfuls and audibly blessed it. It looked like diamonds, rubies, emeralds; he could think of nothing beautiful which it did not resemble. The trees upon the bank were giant garden plants; he noted a definite order in their arrangement, inhaled the fragrance of their blooms. A strange, roseate light shone through the spaces among their trunks and the wind made in their branches the music of aeolian harps. He had no wish to perfect his escape—was content to remain in that enchanting spot until retaken.

A whiz and rattle of grapeshot among the branches high above his head roused him from his dream. The baffled cannoneer had fired him a random farewell. He sprang to his feet, rushed up the sloping bank, and plunged into the forest.

All that day he traveled, laying his course by the rounding sun. The forest seemed interminable; nowhere did he discover a break in it, not even a woodman's road. He had not known that he lived in so wild a region. There was something uncanny in the revelation.

By night fall he was fatigued, footsore, famishing. The thought of his wife and children urged him on. At last he found a road which led him in what he knew to be the right direction. It was as wide and straight as a city street, yet it seemed untraveled. No fields bordered it, no dwelling anywhere. Not so much as the barking of a dog suggested human habitation. The black bodies of the trees formed a straight wall on both sides, terminating on the horizon in a point, like a diagram in a lesson in perspective. Overhead, as he looked up through this rift in the wood, shone great golden stars looking unfamiliar and grouped in strange constellations. He was sure they were arranged in some order which had a secret and malign significance. The wood on either side was full of singular noises, among which—once, twice, and again, he distinctly heard whispers in an unknown tongue.

His neck was in pain and lifting his hand to it he found it horribly swollen. He knew that it had a circle of black where the rope had bruised it. His eyes felt congested; he could no longer close them. His tongue was swollen with thirst; he relieved its fever by thrusting it forward from between his teeth into the cold air. How softly the turf had carpeted the untraveled avenue—he could no longer feel the roadway beneath his feet!

Doubtless, despite his suffering, he had fallen asleep while walking, for now he sees another scene—perhaps he has merely recovered from a delirium. He stands at the gate of his own home. All is as he left it, and all bright and beautiful in the morning sunshine. He must have traveled the entire night. As he pushes open the gate and passes up the wide white walk, he sees a flutter of female garments; his wife, looking fresh and cool and sweet, steps down from the veranda to meet him. At the bottom of the steps she stands waiting, with a smile of ineffable joy, an attitude of matchless grace and dignity. Ah, how beautiful she is! He springs forward with extended arms. As he is about to clasp her he feels a stunning blow upon the back of the neck; a blinding white light blazes all about him with a sound like the shock of a cannon—then all is darkness and silence!

Peyton Farquhar was dead; his body, with a broken neck, swung gently from side to side beneath the timbers of the Owl Creek bridge.

A Son of the Gods

A Study in the Present Tense

A breezy day and a sunny landscape. An open country to right and left and forward; behind, a wood. In the edge of this wood, facing the open but not venturing into it, long lines of troops, halted. The wood is alive with them, and full of confused noises—the occasional rattle of wheels as a battery of artillery goes into position to cover the advance; the hum and murmur of the soldiers talking; a sound of innumerable feet in the dry leaves that strew the interspaces among the trees; hoarse commands of officers. Detached groups of horsemen are well in front—not altogether exposed—many of them intently regarding the crest of a hill a mile away in the direction of the interrupted advance. For this powerful army, moving in battle order through a forest, has met with a formidable obstacle—the open country. The crest of that gentle hill a mile away has a sinister look; it says, Beware! Along it runs a stone wall extending to left and right a great distance. Behind the wall is a hedge; behind the hedge are seen the tops of trees in rather straggling order. Among the trees—what? It is necessary to know.

Yesterday, and for many days and nights previously, we were fighting somewhere; always there was cannonading, with occasional keen rattlings of musketry, mingled with cheers, our own or the enemy's, we seldom knew, attesting some temporary advantage. This morning at daybreak the enemy was gone. We have moved forward across his earthworks, across which we have so often vainly attempted to move before, through the débris of his abandoned camps, among the graves of his fallen, into the woods beyond.

How curiously we had regarded everything! how odd it all had
seemed! Nothing had appeared quite familiar; the most commonplace objects—an old saddle, a splintered wheel, a forgotten can-
teen—everything had related something of the mysterious personality of those strange men who had been killing us. The soldier
never becomes wholly familiar with the conception of his foes as
men like himself; he cannot divest himself of the feeling that they
are another order of beings, differently conditioned, in an environment not altogether of the earth. The smallest vestiges of them rivet
his attention and engage his interest. He thinks of them as inaccessible; and, catching an unexpected glimpse of them, they appear
farther away, and therefore larger, than they really are—like objects
in a fog. He is somewhat in awe of them.

From the edge of the wood leading up the acclivity are the tracks
of horses and wheels—the wheels of cannon. The yellow grass is
beaten down by the feet of infantry. Clearly they have passed this
way in thousands; they have not withdrawn by the country roads.
This is significant—it is the difference between retiring and
retreating.

That group of horsemen is our commander, his staff and escort.
He is facing the distant crest, holding his field-glass against his eyes
with both hands, his elbows needlessly elevated. It is a fashion; it
seems to dignify the act; we are all addicted to it. Suddenly he lowers the glass and says a few words to those about him. Two or three
aides detach themselves from the group and canter away into the
woods, along the lines in each direction. We did not hear his words,
but we know them: "Tell General X. to send forward the skirmish
line." Those of us who have been out of place resume our positions;
the men resting at ease straighten themselves and the ranks are re-
formed without a command. Some of us staff officers dismount and
look at our saddle girths; those already on the ground remount.

Galloping rapidly along in the edge of the open ground comes a
young officer on a snow-white horse. His saddle blanket is scarlet.
What a fool! No one who has ever been in action but remembers
how naturally every rifle turns toward the man on a white horse;
no one but has observed how a bit of red enrages the bull of battle.
That such colors are fashionable in military life must be accepted

as the most astonishing of all the phenomena of human vanity. They would seem to have been devised to increase the death-rate.

This young officer is in full uniform, as if on parade. He is all agleam with bullion—a blue-and-gold edition of the Poetry of War. A wave of derisive laughter runs abreast of him all along the line. But how handsome he is!—with what careless grace he sits his horse!

He reins up within a respectful distance of the corps commander and salutes. The old soldier nods familiarly; he evidently knows him. A brief colloquy between them is going on; the young man seems to be preferring some request which the elder one is indisposed to grant. Let us ride a little nearer. Ah! too late—it is ended. The young officer salutes again, wheels his horse, and rides straight toward the crest of the hill!

A thin line of skirmishers, the men deployed at six paces or so apart, now pushes from the wood into the open. The commander speaks to his bugler, who claps his instrument to his lips. *Tra-la-la! Tra-la-la!* The skirmishers halt in their tracks.

Meantime the young horseman has advanced a hundred yards. He is riding at a walk, straight up the long slope, with never a turn of the head. How glorious! Gods! what would we not give to be in his place—with his soul! He does not draw his sabre; his right hand hangs easily at his side. The breeze catches the plume in his hat and flutters it smartly. The sunshine rests upon his shoulder-straps, lovingly, like a visible benediction. Straight on he rides. Ten thousand pairs of eyes are fixed upon him with an intensity that he can hardly fail to feel; ten thousand hearts keep quick time to the inaudible hoof-beats of his snowy steed. He is not alone—he draws all souls after him. But we remember that we laughed! On and on, straight for the hedge-lined wall, he rides. Not a look backward. O, if he would but turn—if he could but see the love, the adoration, the atonement!

Not a word is spoken; the populous depths of the forest still murmur with their unseen and unseeing swarm, but all along the fringe is silence. The burly commander is an equestrian statue of himself. The mounted staff officers, their field-glasses up, are motionless all. The line of battle in the edge of the wood stands at a new kind of "attention," each man in the attitude in which he was caught by the consciousness of what is going on. All these hardened and impenitent man-killers, to whom death in its awfulest forms is a fact familiar to their every-day observation; who sleep on hills trembling with the thunder of great guns, dine in the midst of streaming missiles, and play at cards among the dead faces of their dearest friends—all are watching with suspended breath and beating hearts the outcome of an act involving the life of one man. Such is the magnetism of courage and devotion.

If now you should turn your head you would see a simultaneous movement among the spectators—a start, as if they had received an electric shock—and looking forward again to the now distant horseman you would see that he has in that instant altered his direction and is riding at an angle to his former course. The spectators suppose the sudden deflection to be caused by a shot, perhaps a wound; but take this field-glass and you will observe that he is riding toward a break in the wall and hedge. He means, if not killed, to ride through and overlook the country beyond.

You are not to forget the nature of this man's act; it is not permitted to you to think of it as an instance of bravado, nor, on the other hand, a needless sacrifice of self. If the enemy has not retreated he is in force on that ridge. The investigator will encounter nothing less than a line-of-battle; there is no need of pickets, videttes, skirmishers, to give warning of our approach; our attacking lines will be visible, conspicuous, exposed to an artillery fire that will shave the ground the moment they break from cover, and for half the distance to a sheet of rifle bullets in which nothing can live. In short, if the enemy is there, it would be madness to attack him in front; he must be manoeuvred out by the immemorial plan of threatening his line of communication, as necessary to his existence as to the diver at the bottom of the sea his air tube. But how ascertain if the enemy is there? There is but one way,—somebody must go and see. The natural and customary thing to do is to send forward a line of skirmishers. But in this case they will answer in the affirmative with all their lives; the enemy, crouching in double ranks behind the stone wall and in cover of the hedge, will wait until it is possible to count each assailant's teeth. At the first volley a half of the questioning line will fall, the other half before it can accomplish the predestined retreat. What a price to pay for gratified curiosity! At what a dear rate an army must sometimes purchase knowledge! "Let me pay all," says this gallant man—this military Christ!

There is no hope except the hope against hope that the crest is clear. True, he might prefer capture to death. So long as he advances, the line will not fire—why should it? He can safely ride into the hostile ranks and become a prisoner of war. But this would defeat his object. It would not answer our question; it is necessary either that he return unharmed or be shot to death before our eyes. Only so shall we know how to act. If captured—why, that might have been done by a half-dozen stragglers.

Now begins an extraordinary contest of intellect between a man and an army. Our horseman, now within a quarter of a mile of the crest, suddenly wheels to the left and gallops in a direction parallel to it. He has caught sight of his antagonist; he knows all. Some slight advantage of ground has enabled him to overlook a part of the line. If he were here he could tell us in words. But that is now hopeless; he must make the best use of the few minutes of life remaining to him, by compelling the enemy himself to tell us as much and as plainly as possible—which, naturally, that discreet power is reluctant to do. Not a rifleman in those crouching ranks, not a cannoneer at those masked and shotted guns, but knows the needs of the situation, the imperative duty of forbearance. Besides, there has been time enough to forbid them all to fire. True, a single rifle-shot might drop him and be no great disclosure. But firing is infectious—and see how rapidly he moves, with never a pause except as he whirls his horse about to take a new direction, never directly backward toward us, never directly forward toward his executioners. All this is visible through the glass; it seems occurring within pistol-shot; we see all but the enemy, whose presence, whose thoughts, whose motives we infer. To the unaided eye there is nothing but a black figure on a white horse, tracing slow zigzags against the slope of a distant hill—so slowly they seem almost to creep.

Now—the glass again—he has tired of his failure, or sees his error, or has gone mad; he is dashing directly forward at the wall, as if to take it at a leap, hedge and all! One moment only and he wheels right about and is speeding like the wind straight down the slope—toward his friends, toward his death! Instantly the wall is topped with a fierce roll of smoke for a distance of hundreds of yards to right and left. This is as instantly dissipated by the wind, and before the rattle of the rifles reaches us he is down. No, he recovers his seat; he has but pulled his horse upon its haunches. They are up and away! A tremendous cheer bursts from our ranks, relieving the insupportable tension of our feelings. And the horse and its rider? Yes, they are up and away. Away, indeed—they are making directly to our left, parallel to the now steadily blazing and smoking wall. The rattle of the musketry is continuous, and every bullet's target is that courageous heart.

Suddenly a great bank of white smoke pushes upward from behind the wall. Another and another—a dozen roll up before the thunder of the explosions and the humming of the missiles reach our ears and the missiles themselves come bounding through clouds of dust into our covert, knocking over here and there a man and causing a temporary distraction, a passing thought of self.

The dust drifts away. Incredible!—that enchanted horse and rider have passed a ravine and are climbing another slope to unveil another conspiracy of silence, to thwart the will of another armed host. Another moment and that crest too is in eruption. The horse rears and strikes the air with its forefeet. They are down at last. But look again—the man has detached himself from the dead animal. He stands erect, motionless, holding his sabre in his right hand straight above his head. His face is toward us. Now he lowers his hand to a level with his face and moves it outward, the blade of the sabre describing a downward curve. It is a sign to us, to the world, to posterity. It is a hero's salute to death and history.

Again the spell is broken; our men attempt to cheer; they are choking with emotion; they utter hoarse, discordant cries; they clutch their weapons and press tumultuously forward into the open. The skirmishers, without orders, against orders, are going forward at a keen run, like hounds unleashed. Our cannon speak and the enemy's now open in full chorus; to right and left as far as we can see, the distant crest, seeming now so near, erects its towers of cloud and the great shot pitch roaring down among our moving masses. Flag after flag of ours emerges from the wood, line after line sweeps forth, catching the sunlight on its burnished arms. The rear battalions alone are in obedience; they preserve their proper distance from the insurgent front.

The commander has not moved. He now removes his field-glass from his eyes and glances to the right and left. He sees the human current flowing on either side of him and his huddled escort, like tide waves parted by a rock. Not a sign of feeling in his face; he is thinking. Again he directs his eyes forward; they slowly traverse that malign and awful crest. He addresses a calm word to his bugler. *Tra-la-la! Tra-la-la!* The injunction has an imperiousness which enforces it. It is repeated by all the bugles of all the subordinate commanders; the sharp metallic notes assert themselves above the hum of the advance and penetrate the sound of the cannon. To halt is to withdraw. The colors move slowly back; the lines face about and sullenly follow, bearing their wounded; the skirmishers return, gathering up the dead.

Ah, those many, many needless dead! That great soul whose beautiful body is lying over yonder, so conspicuous against the sere hillside—could it not have been spared the bitter consciousness of a vain devotion? Would one exception have marred too much the pitiless perfection of the divine, eternal plan?

The Affair at Coulter's Notch

"Do you think, Colonel, that your brave Coulter would like to put one of his guns in here?" the general asked.

He was apparently not altogether serious; it certainly did not seem a place where any artillerist, however brave, would like to put a gun. The colonel thought that possibly his division commander meant good-humoredly to intimate that in a recent conversation between them Captain Coulter's courage had been too highly extolled.

"General," he replied warmly, "Coulter would like to put a gun anywhere within reach of those people," with a motion of his hand in the direction of the enemy.

"It is the only place," said the general. He was serious, then.

The place was a depression, a "notch," in the sharp crest of a hill. It was a pass, and through it ran a turnpike, which reaching this highest point in its course by a sinuous ascent through a thin forest made a similar, though less steep, descent toward the enemy. For a mile to the left and a mile to the right, the ridge, though occupied by Federal infantry lying close behind the sharp crest and appearing as if held in place by atmospheric pressure, was inaccessible to artillery. There was no place but the bottom of the notch, and that was barely wide enough for the roadbed. From the Confederate side this point was commanded by two batteries posted on a slightly lower elevation beyond a creek, and a half-mile away. All the guns but one were masked by the trees of an orchard; that one—it seemed a bit of impudence—was on an open lawn directly in front of a rather grandiose building, the planter's dwelling. The gun was safe enough in its exposure—but only because the Federal infantry had been forbidden to fire. Coulter's Notch—it came to be called so—was not, that pleasant summer afternoon, a place where one would "like to put a gun."

Three or four dead horses lay there sprawling in the road, three or four dead men in a trim row at one side of it, and a little back, down the hill. All but one were cavalrymen belonging to the Federal advance. One was a quartermaster. The general commanding the division and the colonel commanding the brigade, with their staffs and escorts, had ridden into the notch to have a look at the enemy's guns—which had straightway obscured themselves in towering clouds of smoke. It was hardly profitable to be curious about guns which had the trick of the cuttlefish, and the season of observation had been brief. At its conclusion—a short remove backward from where it began—occurred the conversation already partly reported. "It is the only place," the general repeated thoughtfully, "to get at them."

The colonel looked at him gravely. "There is room for only one gun, General—one against twelve."

"That is true—for only one at a time," said the commander with something like, yet not altogether like, a smile. "But then, your brave Coulter—a whole battery in himself."

The tone of irony was now unmistakable. It angered the colonel, but he did not know what to say. The spirit of military subordination is not favorable to retort, nor even to deprecation.

At this moment a young officer of artillery came riding slowly up the road attended by his bugler. It was Captain Coulter. He could not have been more than twenty-three years of age. He was of medium height, but very slender and lithe, and sat his horse with something of the air of a civilian. In face he was of a type singularly unlike the men about him; thin, high-nosed, gray-eyed, with a slight blond mustache, and long, rather straggling hair of the same color. There was an apparent negligence in his attire. His cap was worn with the visor a trifle askew; his coat was buttoned only at the sword-belt, showing a considerable expanse of white shirt, tolerably clean for that stage of the campaign. But the negligence was all in his dress and bearing; in his face was a look of intense interest in his surroundings. His gray eyes, which seemed occasionally to strike right and left across the landscape, like search-lights, were for the most part fixed upon the sky beyond the Notch; until he should arrive at the summit of the road there was nothing else in that direction to see. As he came opposite his division and brigade commanders at the roadside he saluted mechanically and was about to pass on. The colonel signed to him to halt.

"Captain Coulter," he said, "the enemy has twelve pieces over there on the next ridge. If I rightly understand the general, he directs that you bring up a gun and engage them."

There was a blank silence; the general looked stolidly at a distant regiment swarming slowly up the hill through rough undergrowth, like a torn and draggled cloud of blue smoke; the captain appeared not to have observed him. Presently the captain spoke, slowly and with apparent effort:

"On the next ridge, did you say, sir? Are the guns near the house?"

"Ah, you have been over this road before. Directly at the house."

"And it is—necessary—to engage them? The order is imperative?"

His voice was husky and broken. He was visibly paler. The colonel was astonished and mortified. He stole a glance at the commander. In that set, immobile face was no sign; it was as hard as bronze. A moment later the general rode away, followed by his staff and escort. The colonel, humiliated and indignant, was about to order Captain Coulter in arrest, when the latter spoke a few words in a low tone to his bugler, saluted, and rode straight forward into the Notch, where, presently, at the summit of the road, his fieldglass at his eyes, he showed against the sky, he and his horse, sharply defined and statuesque. The bugler had dashed down the speed and disappeared behind a wood. Presently his bugle was heard singing in the cedars, and in an incredibly short time a single gun with its caisson, each drawn by six horses and manned by its full complement of gunners, came bounding and banging up the grade in a storm of dust, unlimbered under cover, and was run forward by hand to the fatal crest among the dead horses. A gesture of the captain's arm, some strangely agile movements of the men in loading, and almost before the troops along the way had ceased to hear the rattle of the wheels, a great white cloud sprang forward down the slope, and with a deafening report the affair at Coulter's Notch had begun.

It is not intended to relate in detail the progress and incidents of that ghastly contest—a contest without vicissitudes, its alternations only different degrees of despair. Almost at the instant when Captain Coulter's gun blew its challenging cloud twelve answering clouds rolled upward from among the trees about the plantation house, a deep multiple report roared back like a broken echo, and thenceforth to the end the Federal cannoneers fought their hopeless battle in an atmosphere of living iron whose thoughts were lightnings and whose deeds were death.

Unwilling to see the efforts which he could not aid and the slaughter which he could not stay, the colonel ascended the ridge at a point a quarter of a mile to the left, whence the Notch, itself invisible, but pushing up successive masses of smoke, seemed the crater of a volcano in thundering eruption. With his glass he watched the enemy's guns, noting as he could the effects of Coulter's fire—if Coulter still lived to direct it. He saw that the Federal gunners, ignoring those of the enemy's pieces whose positions could be determined by their smoke only, gave their whole attention to the one that maintained its place in the open—the lawn in front of the house. Over and about that hardy piece the shells exploded at intervals of a few seconds. Some exploded in the house, as could be seen by thin ascensions of smoke from the breached roof. Figures of prostrate men and horses were plainly visible.

"If our fellows are doing so good work with a single gun," said the colonel to an aide who happened to be nearest, "they must be suffering like the devil from twelve. Go down and present the commander of that piece with my congratulations on the accuracy of his fire."

Turning to his adjutant-general he said, "Did you observe Coulter's damned reluctance to obey orders?"

"Yes, sir, I did."

"Well, say nothing about it, please. I don't think the general will care to make any accusations. He will probably have enough to do in explaining his own connection with this uncommon way of amusing the rear-guard of a retreating enemy."

A young officer approached from below, climbing breathless up the acclivity. Almost before he had saluted, he gasped out:

"Colonel, I am directed by Colonel Harmon to say that the enemy's guns are within easy reach of our rifles, and most of them visible from several points along the ridge."

The brigade commander looked at him without a trace of interest in his expression. "I know it," he said quietly.

The young adjutant was visibly embarrassed. "Colonel Harmon would like to have permission to silence those guns," he stammered.

"So should I," the colonel said in the same tone. "Present my compliments to Colonel Harmon and say to him that the general's orders for the infantry not to fire are still in force."

The adjutant saluted and retired. The colonel ground his heel into the earth and turned to look again at the enemy's guns.

"Colonel," said the adjutant-general, "I don't know that I ought to say anything, but there is something wrong in all this. Do you happen to know that Captain Coulter is from the South?"

"No; *was* he, indeed?"

"I heard that last summer the division which the general then commanded was in the vicinity of Coulter's home—camped there for weeks, and——"

"Listen!" said the colonel, interrupting with an upward gesture. "Do you hear *that*?"

"That" was the silence of the Federal gun. The staff, the orderlies, the lines of infantry behind the crest—all had "heard," and were looking curiously in the direction of the crater, whence no smoke now ascended except desultory cloudlets from the enemy's shells. Then came the blare of a bugle, a faint rattle of wheels; a minute later the sharp reports recommenced with double activity. The demolished gun had been replaced with a sound one.

"Yes," said the adjutant-general, resuming his narrative, "the general made the acquaintance of Coulter's family. There was trouble—I don't know the exact nature of it—something about Coulter's wife. She is a red-hot Secessionist, as they all are, except Coulter himself, but she is a good wife and high-bred lady. There was a complaint to army headquarters. The general was transferred to this division. It is odd that Coulter's battery should afterward have been assigned to it."

The colonel had risen from the rock upon which they had been sitting. His eyes were blazing with a generous indignation.

"See here, Morrison," said he, looking his gossiping staff officer straight in the face, "did you get that story from a gentleman or a liar?"

"I don't want to say how I got it, Colonel, unless it is necessary"—he was blushing a trifle—"but I'll stake my life upon its truth in the main."

The colonel turned toward a small knot of officers some distance away. "Lieutenant Williams!" he shouted.

One of the officers detached himself from the group and coming forward saluted, saying: "Pardon me, Colonel, I thought you had been informed. Williams is dead down there by the gun. What can I do, sir?"

Lieutenant Williams was the aide who had had the pleasure of conveying to the officer in charge of the gun his brigade commander's congratulations.

"Go," said the colonel, "and direct the withdrawal of that gun instantly. No—I'll go myself."

He strode down the declivity toward the rear of the Notch at a break-neck pace, over rocks and through brambles, followed by his little retinue in tumultuous disorder. At the foot of the declivity they mounted their waiting animals and took to the road at a lively trot, round a bend and into the Notch. The spectacle which they encountered there was appalling!

Within that defile, barely broad enough for a single gun, were piled the wrecks of no fewer than four. They had noted the silencing of only the last one disabled—there had been a lack of men to replace it quickly with another. The debris lay on both sides of the road; the men had managed to keep an open way between, through which the fifth piece was now firing. The men?—they looked like demons of the pit! All were hatless, all stripped to the waist, their reeking skins black with blotches of powder and spattered with gouts of blood. They worked like madmen, with rammer and cartridge, lever and lanyard. They set their swollen shoulders and bleeding hands against the wheels at each recoil and heaved the heavy gun back to its place. There were no commands; in that awful environment of whooping shot, exploding shells, shrieking fragments of iron, and flying splinters of wood, none could have been heard. Officers, if officers there were, were indistinguishable; all worked together—each while he lasted—governed by the eye. When the gun was sponged, it was loaded; when loaded, aimed and fired. The colonel observed something new to his military experience—something horrible and unnatural: the gun was bleeding at the mouth! In temporary default of water, the man sponging had dipped his sponge into a pool of comrade's blood. In all this work there was no clashing; the duty of the instant was obvious. When one fell, another, looking a trifle cleaner, seemed to rise from the earth in the dead man's tracks, to fall in his turn.

With the ruined guns lay the ruined men—alongside the wreckage, under it and atop of it; and back down the road—a ghastly procession!—crept on hands and knees such of the wounded as were able to move. The colonel—he had compassionately sent his cavalcade to the right about—had to ride over those who were entirely dead in order not to crush those who were partly alive. Into that hell he tranquilly held his way, rode up alongside the gun, and, in the obscurity of the last discharge, tapped upon the cheek the man holding the rammer—who straightway fell, thinking himself killed. A fiend seven times damned sprang out of the smoke to take his place, but paused and gazed up at the mounted officer with an unearthly regard, his teeth flashing between his black lips, his eyes, fierce and expanded, burning like coals beneath his bloody brow. The colonel made an authoritative gesture and pointed to the rear. The fiend bowed in token of obedience. It was Captain Coulter.

Simultaneously with the colonel's arresting sign, silence fell upon the whole field of action. The procession of missiles no longer streamed into that defile of death, for the enemy also had ceased firing. His army had been gone for hours, and the commander of his rear-guard, who had held his position perilously long in hope to silence the Federal fire, at that strange moment had silenced his own. "I was not aware of the breadth of my authority," said the colonel to anybody, riding forward to the crest to see what had really happened.

An hour later his brigade was in bivouac on the enemy's ground, and its idlers were examining, with something of awe, as the faithful inspect a saint's relics, a score of straddling dead horses and three disabled guns, all spiked. The fallen men had been carried away; their torn and broken bodies would have given too great satisfaction.

Naturally, the colonel established himself and his military family in the plantation house. It was somewhat shattered, but it was better than the open air. The furniture was greatly deranged and broken. Walls and ceilings were knocked away here and there, and a lingering odor of powder smoke was everywhere. The beds, the closets of women's clothing, the cupboards were not greatly damaged. The new tenants for a night made themselves comfortable, and the virtual effacement of Coulter's battery supplied them with an interesting topic.

During supper an orderly of the escort showed himself into the dining-room and asked permission to speak to the colonel.

"What is it, Barbour?" said that officer pleasantly, having overheard the request.

"Colonel, there is something wrong in the cellar; I don't know what—somebody there. I was down there rummaging about."

"I will go down and see," said a staff officer, rising.

"So will I," the colonel said; "let the others remain. Lead on, orderly."

They took a candle from the table and descended the cellar stairs, the orderly in visible trepidation. The candle made but a feeble light, but presently, as they advanced, its narrow circle of illumination revealed a human figure seated on the ground against the black stone wall which they were skirting, its knees elevated, its head bowed sharply forward. The face, which should have been seen in profile, was invisible, for the man was bent so far forward that his long hair concealed it; and, strange to relate, the beard, of a much darker hue, fell in a great tangled mass and lay along the ground at his side. They involuntarily paused; then the colonel, taking the candle from the orderly's shaking hand, approached the man and attentively considered him. The long dark beard was the hair of a woman—dead. The dead woman clasped in her arms a dead babe. Both were clasped in the arms of the man, pressed against his breast, against his lips. There was blood in the hair of the woman; there was blood in the hair of the man. A yard away, near an irregular depression in the beaten earth which formed the cellar's floor—a fresh excavation with a convex bit of iron, having jagged edges, visible in one of the sides—lay an infant's foot. The colonel held the light as high as he could. The floor of the room above was broken through, the splinters pointing at all angles downward. "This casemate is not bomb-proof," said the colonel gravely. It did not occur to him that his summing up of the matter had any levity in it.

They stood about the group awhile in silence; the staff officer was thinking of his unfinished supper, the orderly of what might possibly be in one of the casks on the other side of the cellar. Suddenly the man whom they had thought dead raised his head and gazed tranquilly into their faces. His complexion was coal black; the cheeks were apparently tattooed in irregular sinuous lines from the eyes downward. The lips, too, were white, like those of a stage negro. There was blood upon his forehead.

The staff officer drew back a pace, the orderly two paces.

"What are you doing here, my man?" said the colonel unmoved.

"This house belongs to me, sir," was the reply, civilly delivered.

"To you? Ah, I see! And these?"

"My wife and child. I am Captain Coulter."

Jupiter Doke, Brigadier-General

From the Secretary of War to the Hon. Jupiter Doke, Hardpan Crossroads, Posey County, Illinois.

WASHINGTON, *November 3, 1861.*
Having faith in your patriotism and ability, the President has been pleased to appoint you a brigadier-general of volunteers. Do you accept?

From the Hon. Jupiter Doke to the Secretary of War.

HARDPAN, ILLINOIS, *November 9, 1861.*
It is the proudest moment of my life. The office is one which should be neither sought nor declined. In times that try men's souls the patriot knows no North, no South, no East, no West. His motto should be: "My country, my whole country and nothing but my country." I accept the great trust confided in me by a free and intelligent people, and with a firm reliance on the principles of constitutional liberty, and invoking the guidance of an all-wise Providence, Ruler of Nations, shall labor so to discharge it as to leave no blot upon my political escutcheon. Say to his Excellency, the successor of the immortal Washington in the Seat of Power, that the patronage of my office will be bestowed with an eye single to securing the greatest good to the greatest number, the stability of republican institutions and the triumph of the party in all elections; and to this I pledge my life, my fortune and my sacred honor. I shall at once prepare an appropriate response to the speech of the chairman of the committee deputed to inform me of my appointment, and I trust the sentiments therein

*expressed will strike a sympathetic chord in the public heart, as
well as command the Executive approval.*

From the Secretary of War to Major-General Blount Wardorg,
Commanding the Military Department of Eastern Kentucky.

WASHINGTON, *November 14, 1861.*
*I have assigned to your department Brigadier-General Jupiter
Doke, who will soon proceed to Distilleryville, on the Little
Buttermilk River, and take command of the Illinois Brigade at
that point, reporting to you by letter for orders. Is the route from
Covington by way of Bluegrass, Opossum Corners and Horsecave
still infested with bushwackers, as reported in your last dispatch? I
have a plan for cleaning them out.*

From Major-General Blount Wardorg to the Secretary of War.

LOUISVILLE, KENTUCKY, *November 20, 1861.*
*The name and services of Brigadier-General Doke are unfamiliar
to me, but I shall be pleased to have the advantage of his skill. The
route from Covington to Distilleryville via Opossum Corners and
Horsecave I have been compelled to abandon to the enemy, whose
guerilla warfare made it possible to keep it open without detaching
too many troops from the front. The brigade at Distilleryville is
supplied by steamboats up the Little Buttermilk.*

From the Secretary of War to Brigadier-General Jupiter Doke,
Hardpan, Illinois.

WASHINGTON, *November 26, 1861.*
*I deeply regret that your commission had been forwarded by mail
before the receipt of your letter of acceptance; so we must dispense
with the formality of official notification to you by a committee.
The President is highly gratified by the noble and patriotic sentiments of your letter, and directs that you proceed at once to your
command at Distilleryville, Kentucky, and there report by letter to
Major-General Wardorg at Louisville, for orders. It is important
that the strictest secrecy be observed regarding your movements*

*until you have passed Covington, as it is desired to hold the enemy
in front of Distilleryville until you are within three days of him.
Then if your approach is known it will operate as a demonstration
against his right and cause him to strengthen it with his left now
at Memphis, Tennessee, which it is desirable to capture first. Go by
way of Bluegrass, Opossum Corners and Horsecave. All officers
are expected to be in full uniform when en route to the front.*

From Brigadier-General Jupiter Doke to the Secretary of War.

COVINGTON, KENTUCKY, *December 7, 1861.*

*I arrived yesterday at this point, and have given my proxy to Joel
Briller, Esq., my wife's cousin, and a staunch Republican, who will
worthily represent Posey County in field and forum. He points
with pride to a stainless record in the halls of legislation, which
have often echoed to his soul-stirring eloquence on questions which
lie at the very foundation of popular government. He has been
called the Patrick Henry of Hardpan, where he has done yeoman's
service in the cause of civil and religious liberty. Mr. Briller left for
Distilleryville last evening, and the standard bearer of the
Democratic host confronting that stronghold of freedom will find
him a lion in his path. I have been asked to remain here and
deliver some addresses to the people in a local contest involving
issues of paramount importance. That duty being performed, I
shall in person enter the arena of armed debate and move in the
direction of the heaviest firing, burning my ships behind me. I forward by this mail to his Excellency the President a request for the
appointment of my son, Jabez Leonidas Doke, as postmaster at
Hardpan. I would take it, sir, as a great favor if you would give
the application a strong oral indorsement, as the appointment is in
the line of reform. Be kind enough to inform me what are the
emoluments of the office I hold in the military arm, and if they are
by salary or fees. Are there any perquisites? My mileage account
will be transmitted monthly.*

From Brigadier-General Jupiter Doke to Major General Blount
Wardorg.

DISTILLERYVILLE, KENTUCKY, *January 12, 1862.*
I arrived on the tented field yesterday by steamboat, the recent
storms having inundated the landscape, covering, I understand, the
greater part of a congressional district. I am pained to find that
Joel Briller, Esq., a prominent citizen of Posey County, Illinois, and
a far-seeing statesman who held my proxy, and who a month ago
should have been thundering at the gates of Disunion, has not
been heard from, and has doubtless been sacrificed upon the altar
of his country. In him the American people lose a bulwark of free-
dom. I would respectfully move that you designate a committee to
draw up resolutions of respect to his memory, and that the office
holders and men under your command wear the usual badge of
mourning for thirty days. I shall at once place myself at the head of
affairs here, and am now ready to entertain any suggestions which
you may make, looking to the better enforcement of the laws in this
commonwealth. The militant Democrats on the other side of the
river appear to be contemplating extreme measures. They have two
large cannons facing this way, and yesterday morning, I am told,
some of them came down to the water's edge and remained in ses-
sion for some time, making infamous allegations.

From the Diary of Brigadier-General Jupiter Doke, at
Distilleryville, Kentucky.

January 12, 1862.—*On my arrival yesterday at the Henry Clay*
Hotel (named in honor of the late far-seeing statesman) I was
waited on by a delegation consisting of the three colonels intrusted
with the command of the regiments of my brigade. It was an occa-
sion that will be memorable in the political annals of America.
Forwarded copies of the speeches to the Posey Maverick, *to be*
spread upon the record of the ages. The gentlemen composing the
delegation unanimously reaffirmed their devotion to the principles
of national unity and the Republican party. Was gratified to
recognize in them men of political prominence and untarnished
escutcheons. At the subsequent banquet, sentiments of lofty

patriotism were expressed. Wrote to Mr. Wardorg at Louisville for instructions.

January 13, 1862.—Leased a prominent residence (the former incumbent being absent in arms against his country) for the term of one year, and wrote at once for Mrs. Brigadier-General Doke and the vital issues—excepting Jabez Leonidas. In the camp of treason opposite here there are supposed to be three thousand misguided men laying the ax at the root of the tree of liberty. They have a clear majority, many of our men having returned without leave to their constituents. We could probably not poll more than two thousand votes. Have advised my heads of regiments to make a canvass of those remaining, all bolters to be read out of the phalanx.

January 14, 1862.—Wrote to the President, asking for the contract to supply this command with firearms and regalia through my brother-in-law, prominently identified with the manufacturing interests of the country. Club of cannon soldiers arrived at Jayhawk, three miles back from here, on their way to join us in battle array. Marched my whole brigade to Jayhawk to escort them into town, but their chairman, mistaking us for the opposing party, opened fire on the head of the procession and by the extraordinary noise of the cannon balls (I had no conception of it!) so frightened my horse that I was unseated without a contest. The meeting adjourned in disorder and returning to camp I found that a deputation of the enemy had crossed the river in our absence and made a division of the loaves and fishes. Wrote to the President, applying for the Gubernatorial Chair of the Territory of Idaho.

From Editorial Article in the Posey, Illinois, "Maverick," January 20, 1862.

Brigadier-General Doke's thrilling account, in another column, of the Battle of Distilleryville will make the heart of every loyal Illinoisian leap with exultation. The brilliant exploit marks an era in military history, and as General Doke says, "lays broad and deep the foundations of American prowess in arms." As none of the troops engaged, except the gallant author-chieftain (a host in himself) hails from Posey County, he justly considered that a list of the fallen would only occupy our valuable space to the exclusion of more important matter, but his account of the strategic ruse by which he apparently abandoned his camp and so inveigled a perfidious enemy into it for the purpose of murdering the sick, the unfortunate countertempus *at Jayhawk, the subsequent dash upon a trapped enemy flushed with a supposed success, driving their terrified legions across an impassable river which precluded pursuit—all these "moving accidents by flood and field" are related with a pen of fire and have all the terrible interest of romance.*

Verily, truth is stranger than fiction and the pen is mightier than the sword. When by the graphic power of the art preservative of all arts we are brought face to face with such glorious events as these, the Maverick's *enterprise in securing for its thousands of readers the services of so distinguished a contributor as the Great Captain who made the history as well as wrote it seems a matter of almost secondary importance. For President in 1864 (subject to the decision of the Republican National Convention) Brigadier-General Jupiter Doke, of Illinois!*

From Major-General Blount Wardorg to Brigadier-General Jupiter Doke.

LOUISVILLE, *January 22, 1862.*
Your letter apprising me of your arrival at Distilleryville was delayed in transmission, having only just been received (open) through the courtesy of the Confederate department commander under a flag of truce. He begs me to assure you that he would consider it an act of cruelty to trouble you, and I think it would be. Maintain, however a threatening attitude, but at the least pressure retire. Your position is simply an outpost which it is not intended to hold.

From Major-General Blount Wardorg to the Secretary of War.

LOUISVILLE, *January 23, 1862.*
I have certain information that the enemy has concentrated twen-
ty thousand troops of all arms on the Little Buttermilk. According
to your assignment, General Doke is in command of the small
brigade of raw troops opposing them. It is no part of my plan to
contest the enemy's advance at that point, but I cannot hold myself
responsible for any reverses to the brigade mentioned, under its
present commander. I think him a fool.

From the Secretary of War to MajorGeneral Blount Wardorg.

WASHINGTON, *February 1, 1862.*
The President has great faith in General Doke. If your estimate of
him is correct, however, he would seem to be singularly well placed
where he now is, as your plans appear to contemplate a consider-
able sacrifice for whatever advantages you expect to gain.

From Brigadier-General Jupiter Doke to Major-General Blount
Wardorg.

DISTILLERYVILLE, *February 1, 1862.*
To-morrow I shall remove my headquarters to Jayhawk in order to
point the way whenever my brigade retires from Distilleryville, as
foreshadowed by your letter of the 22d ult. I have appointed a
Committee on Retreat, the minutes of whose first meeting I trans-
mit to you. You will perceive that the committee having been duly
organized by the election of a chairman and secretary, a resolution
(prepared by myself) was adopted, to the effect that in case treason
again raises her hideous head on this side of the river every man of
the brigade is to mount a mule, the procession to move promptly in
the direction of Louisville and the loyal North. In preparation for
such an emergency I have for some time been collecting mules from
the resident Democracy, and have on hand 2300 in a field at
Jayhawk. Eternal vigilance is the price of liberty!

From Major-General Gibeon J. Buxter, C.S.A., to the Confederate
Secretary of War.

BUNG STATION, KENTUCKY, *February 4, 1862.*
On the night of the 2d inst., our entire force, consisting of 25,000
men and thirty-two field pieces, under command of Major-
General Simmons B. Flood, crossed by a ford to the north side of
Little Buttermilk River at a point three miles from Distilleryville
and moved obliquely down and away from the stream, to strike
the Covington turnpike at Jayhawk; the object being, as you know,
to capture Covington, destroy Cincinnati and occupy the Ohio
Valley. For some months there had been in our front only a small
brigade of undisciplined troops, apparently without a commander,
who were useful to us, for by not disturbing them we could create
an impression of our weakness. But the movement on Jayhawk
having isolated them, I was about to detach an Alabama regiment
to bring them in, my division being the leading one, when an
earth-shaking rumble was felt and heard, and suddenly the head-
of-column was struck by one of the terrible tornadoes for which this
region is famous, and utterly annihilated. The tornado, I believe,
passed along the entire length of the road back to the ford, dispers-
ing or destroying our entire army; but of this I cannot be sure, for I
was lifted from the earth insensible and blown back to the south
side of the river. Continuous firing all night on the north side and
the reports of such of our men as have recrossed at the ford con-
vince me that the Yankee brigade has exterminated the disabled
survivors. Our loss has been uncommonly heavy. Of my own divi-
sion of 15,000 infantry, the casualties—killed, wounded, cap-
tured, and missing—are 14,994. Of General Dolliver Billow's
division, 11,200 strong, I can find but two officers and a nigger
cook. Of the artillery, 800 men, none has reported on this side of
the river. General Flood is dead. I have assumed command of the
expeditionary force, but owing to the heavy losses have deemed it
advisable to contract my line of supplies as rapidly as possible. I
shall push southward to-morrow morning early. The purposes of
the campaign have been as yet but partly accomplished.

From Major-General Dolliver Billows, C.S.A., to the Confederate
Secretary of War.

> BUHAC, KENTUCKY, *February 5, 1862.*
> *...But during the 2d they had, unknown to us, been reinforced by
> fifty thousand cavalry, and being apprised of our movement by a
> spy, this vast body was drawn up in the darkness at Jayhawk, and
> as the head of our column reached that point at about 11 P.M., fell
> upon it with astonishing fury, destroying the division of General
> Buxter in an instant. General Baumschank's brigade of artillery,
> which was in the rear, may have escaped—I did not wait to see,
> but withdrew my division to the river at a point several miles
> above the ford, and at daylight ferried it across on two fence rails
> lashed together with a suspender. Its losses, from an effective
> strength of 11,200, are 11,199. General Buxter is dead. I am
> changing my base to Mobile, Alabama.*

From Brigadier-General Schneddeker Baumschank, C.S.A., to the
Confederate Secretary of War.

> IODINE, KENTUCKY, *February 6, 1862.*
> *...Yoost den somdings occur, I know nod vot it vos—somdings
> mackneefcent, but it vas nod vor—und I finds meinselluf, afder
> leedle viles, in dis blace, midout a hors und mit no men und goons.
> Sheneral Peelows is deadt. You will blease be so goot as to resign
> me—I vights no more in a dam gontry vere I gets yipped und
> knows nod how it vos done.*

Resolutions of Congress, February 15, 1862.

> Resolved, *That the thanks of Congress are due, and hereby ten-
> dered, to Brigadier-General Jupiter Doke and the gallant men
> under his command for their unparalleled feat of attacking—
> themselves only 2000 strong—an army of 25,000 men and
> utterly overthrowing it, killing 5327, making prisoners of 19,003,
> of whom more than half were wounded, taking 32 guns, 20,000
> stand of small arms and, in short, the enemy's entire equipment.*

Resolved, *That for this unexampled victory the President be requested to designate a day of thanksgiving and public celebration of religious rites in the various churches.*

Resolved, *That he be requested, in further commemoration of the great event, and in reward of the gallant spirits whose deeds have added such imperishable lustre to the American arms, to appoint, with the advice and consent of the Senate, the following officer:*

One major-general.

Statement of Mr. Hannibal Alcazar Peyton, of Jayhawk, Kentucky.

Dat wus a almighty dark night, sho', and dese yere ole eyes aint wuf shuks but I's got a year like a sque'l, an' w'en I cotch de mummer o' v'ices I knowed dat gang b'long on de far side o' de ribber. So I jes' runs in de house an' wakes Marse Doke an' tells him: "Skin outer dis fo' yo' life!" An' de Lo'd bress my soul! ef dat man didn' go right fru de winder in his shir' tail an' break for to cross de mule patch! An' dem twenty-free hunerd mules dey jes' t'nk it is de debble hese'f wid de brandin' iron, an' dey bu'st outen dat patch like a yarthquake, an' pile inter de upper ford road, an' flash down it five deep, an' it full o' Confed'rates from en' to en'!...

from The Devil's Dictionary

Preface

The Devil's Dictionary was begun in a weekly paper in 1881, and was continued in a desultory way at long intervals until 1906. In that year a large part of it was published in covers with the title *The Cynic's Word Book*, a name which the author had not the power to reject or happiness to approve. To quote the publishers of the present work:

> *This more reverent title had previously been forced upon him by the religious scruples of the last newspaper in which a part of the work had appeared, with the natural consequence that when it came out in covers the country already had been flooded by its imitators with a score of 'cynic' books —The Cynic's This, The Cynic's That, and The Cynic's t'Other. Most of these books were merely stupid, though some of them added the distinction of silliness. Among them, they brought the word "cynic" into disfavor so deep that any book bearing it was discredited in advance of publication.*

Meantime, too, some of the enterprising humorists of the country had helped themselves to such parts of the work as served their needs, and many of its definitions, anecdotes, phrases and so forth, had become more or less current in popular speech. This explanation is made, not with any pride of priority in trifles, but in simple denial of possible charges of plagiarism, which is no trifle. In merely resuming his own the author hopes to be held guiltless by those to whom the work is addressed —enlightened souls who prefer dry wines to sweet, sense to sentiment, wit to humor and clean English to slang.

A conspicuous, and it is hoped not unpleasant, feature of the book is its abundant illustrative quotations from eminent poets, chief of whom is that learned and ingenius cleric, Father Gassalasca Jape, S.J., whose lines bear his initials. To Father Jape's kindly encouragement and assistance the author of the prose text is greatly indebted.

—*A.B.*

Law & Society

ABASEMENT, n. A decent and customary mental attitude in the presence of wealth or power. Peculiarly appropriate in an employee when addressing an employer.

ACCOMPLICE, n. One associated with another in a crime, having guilty knowledge and complicity, as an attorney who defends a criminal, knowing him guilty. This view of the attorney's position in the matter has not hitherto commanded the assent of attorneys, no one having offered them a fee for assenting.

AMNESTY, n. The state's magnanimity to those offenders whom it would be too expensive to punish.

HABEAS CORPUS. A writ by which a man may be taken out of jail when confined for the wrong crime.

HOMICIDE, n. The slaying of one human being by another. There are four kinds of homicide: felonious, excusable, justifiable, and praiseworthy, but it makes no great difference to the person slain whether he fell by one kind or another — the classification is for advantage of the lawyers.

IDIOT, n. A member of a large and powerful tribe whose influence in human affairs has always been dominant and controlling. The Idiot's activity is not confined to any special field of thought or action, but "pervades and regulates the whole." He has the last word in everything; his decision is unappealable. He sets the fashions of opinion and taste, dictates the limitations of speech and circum-scribes conduct with a dead-line.

IMPARTIAL, adj. Unable to perceive any promise of personal advantage from espousing either side of a controversy or adopting either of two conflicting opinions.

INADMISSIBLE, adj. Not competent to be considered. Said of cer-tain kinds of testimony which juries are supposed to be unfit to be entrusted with, and which judges, therefore, rule out, even of pro-ceedings before themselves alone. Hearsay evidence is inadmissible because the person quoted was unsworn and is not before the court for examination; yet most momentous actions, military, political, commercial and of every other kind, are daily undertaken on hearsay evidence. There is no religion in the world that has any other basis than hearsay evidence. Revelation is hearsay evidence; that the Scriptures are the word of God we have only the testimo-ny of men long dead whose identity is not clearly established and who are not known to have been sworn in any sense. Under the rules of evidence as they now exist in this country, no single asser-tion in the Bible has in its support any evidence admissible in a court of law. It cannot be proved that the battle of Blenheim ever was fought, that there was such a person as Julius Caesar, such an empire as Assyria.

But as records of courts of justice are admissible, it can easily be proved that powerful and malevolent magicians once existed and were a scourge to mankind. The evidence (including confession) upon which certain women were convicted of witchcraft and exe-cuted was without a flaw; it is still unimpeachable. The judges' deci-sions based on it were sound in logic and in law. Nothing in any existing court was ever more thoroughly proved than the charges of witchcraft and sorcery for which so many suffered death. If there were no witches, human testimony and human reason are alike des-titute of value.

JUSTICE, n. A commodity which in a more or less adulterated

condition the State sells to the citizen as a reward for his allegiance, taxes and personal service.

LAND, n. A part of the earth's surface, considered as property. The theory that land is property subject to private ownership and control is the foundation of modern society, and is eminently worthy of the superstructure. Carried to its logical conclusion, it means that some have the right to prevent others from living; for the right to own implies the right exclusively to occupy; and in fact laws of trespass are enacted wherever property in land is recognized. It follows that if the whole area of terra firma is owned by A, B and C, there will be no place for D, E, F and G to be born, or, born as trespassers, to exist.

> *A life on the ocean wave,*
> *A home on the rolling deep,*
> *For the spark the nature gave*
> *I have there the right to keep.*
> *They give me the cat-o'-nine*
> *Whenever I go ashore.*
> *Then ho! for the flashing brine —*
> *I'm a natural commodore! —Dodle*

LAWFUL, adj. Compatible with the will of a judge having jurisdiction.

LAWYER, n. One skilled in circumvention of the law.

LIAR, n. A lawyer with a roving commission.

MONEY, n. A blessing that is of no advantage to us excepting when we part with it. An evidence of culture and a passport to polite society. Supportable property.

NEIGHBOR, n. One whom we are commanded to love as ourselves, and who does all he knows how to make us disobedient.

OATH, n. In law, a solemn appeal to the Deity, made binding upon the conscience by a penalty for perjury.

PARDON, v. To remit a penalty and restore to the life of crime. To add to the lure of crime the temptation of ingratitude.

PLAGIARIZE, v. To take the thought or style of another writer whom one has never, never read.

POLICE, n. An armed force for protection and participation.

PRECEDENT, n. In Law, a previous decision, rule or practice which, in the absence of a definite statute, has whatever force and authority a Judge may choose to give it, thereby greatly simplifying his task of doing as he pleases. As there are precedents for everything, he has only to ignore those that make against his interest and accentuate those in the line of his desire. Invention of the precedent elevates the trial-at-law from the low estate of a fortuitous ordeal to the noble attitude of a dirigible arbitrament.

REASONABLE, adj. Accessible to the infection of our own opinions. Hospitable to persuasion, dissuasion and evasion.

REFORM, v. A thing that mostly satisfies reformers opposed to reformation.

RICH, adj. Holding in trust and subject to an accounting the property of the indolent, the incompetent, the unthrifty, the envious and the luckless. That is the view that prevails in the underworld, where the Brotherhood of Man finds its most logical development and candid advocacy. To denizens of the midworld the word means good and wise.

TAKE, v.t. To acquire, frequently by force but preferably by stealth.

TECHNICALITY, n. In an English court a man named Home was tried for slander in having accused his neighbor of murder. His exact words were: "Sir Thomas Holt hath taken a cleaver and stricken his cook upon the head, so that one side of the head fell upon one shoulder and the other side upon the other shoulder." The defendant was acquitted by instruction of the court, the learned judges holding that the words did not charge murder, for they did not affirm the death of the cook, that being only an inference.

TRIAL, n. A formal inquiry designed to prove and put upon record the blameless characters of judges, advocates and jurors. In order to effect this purpose it is necessary to supply a contrast in the person of one who is called the defendant, the prisoner, or the accused. If the contrast is made sufficiently clear this person is made to undergo such an affliction as will give the virtuous gentlemen a comfortable sense of their immunity, added to that of their worth.

Religion & Politics

ABSOLUTE, adj. Independent, irresponsible. An absolute monarchy is one in which the sovereign does as he pleases so long as he pleases the assassins. Not many absolute monarchies are left, most of them having been replaced by limited monarchies, where the sovereign's power for evil (and for good) is greatly curtailed, and by republics, which are governed by chance.

CHRISTIAN, n. One who believes that the New Testament is a divinely inspired book admirably suited to the spiritual needs of his neighbor. One who follows the teachings of Christ in so far as they are not inconsistent with a life of sin.

I dreamed I stood upon a hill, and, lo!
The godly multitudes walked to and fro
Beneath, in Sabbath garments fitly clad,
With pious mien, appropriately sad,
While all the church bells made a solemn din —
A fire-alarm to those who lived in sin.
Then saw I gazing thoughtfully below,
With tranquil face, upon that holy show
A tall, spare figure in a robe of white,
Whose eyes diffused a melancholy light.
"God keep you, stranger," I exclaimed. "You are
No doubt (your habit shows it) from afar;
And yet I entertain the hope that you,
Like these good people, are a Christian too."
He raised his eyes and with a look so stern
It made me with a thousand blushes burn
Replied —his manner with disdain was spiced:
"What! I a Christian? No, indeed! I'm Christ." —G.J.

CLERGYMAN, n. A man who undertakes the management of our spiritual affairs as a method of bettering his temporal ones.

CONSERVATIVE, n. A statesman who is enamored of existing evils, as distinguished from the Liberal, who wishes to replace them with others.

DIPLOMACY, n. The patriotic art of lying for one's country.

IMPIETY, n. Your irreverence toward my deity.

INCUMBENT, n. A person of the liveliest interest to the outcumbents.

INFLUENCE, n. In politics, a visionary quo given in exchange for a substantial quid.

IRRELIGION, n. The principal one of the great faiths of the world.

PANDEMONIUM, n. Literally, the Place of All the Demons. Most of them have escaped into politics and finance, and the place is now used as a lecture hall by the Audible Reformer. When disturbed by his voice the ancient echoes clamor appropriate responses most gratifying to his pride of distinction.

PANTHEISM, n. The doctrine that everything is God, in contradistinction to the doctrine that God is everything.

PATRIOTISM, n. Combustible rubbish read to the torch of any one ambitious to illuminate his name.

In Dr. Johnson's famous dictionary patriotism is defined as the last resort of a scoundrel. With all due respect to an enlightened but inferior lexicographer I beg to submit that it is the first.

PEACE, n. In international affairs, a period of cheating between two periods of fighting.

> *O, what's the loud uproar assailing*
> *Mine ears without cease?*
> *'Tis the voice of the hopeful, all-hailing*
> *The horrors of peace.*

Ah, Peace Universal; they woo it —
Would marry it, too.
If only they knew how to do it
'Twere easy to do.

They're working by night and by day
On their problem, like moles.
Have mercy, O Heaven, I pray,
On their meddlesome souls! —Ro Amil

PIETY, n. Reverence for the Supreme Being, based upon His supposed resemblance to man.

The pig is taught by sermons and epistles
To think the God of Swine has snout and bristles. —Judibras

POLITICS, n. A strife of interests masquerading as a contest of principles. The conduct of public affairs for private advantage.

POLITICIAN, n. An eel in the fundamental mud upon which the superstructure of organized society is reared. When he wriggles he mistakes the agitation of his tail for the trembling of the edifice. As compared with the statesman, he suffers the disadvantage of being alive.

PRAY, v. To ask that the laws of the universe be annulled in behalf of a single petitioner confessedly unworthy.

PROJECTILE, n. The final arbiter in international disputes. Formerly these disputes were settled by physical contact of the disputants, with such simple arguments as the rudimentary logic of the times could supply — the sword, the spear, and so forth. With the growth of prudence in military affairs the projectile came more and more into favor, and is now held in high esteem by the most courageous. Its capital defect is that it requires personal attendance at the point of propulsion.

PROVIDENTIAL, adj. Unexpectedly and conspicuously beneficial to the person so describing it.

QUORUM, n. A sufficient number of members of a deliberative body to have their own way and their own way of having it. In the United States Senate a quorum consists of the chairman of the Committee on Finance and a messenger from the White House; in the House of Representatives, of the Speaker and the devil.

RABBLE, n. In a republic, those who exercise a supreme authority tempered by fraudulent elections.

RADICALISM, n. The conservatism of to-morrow injected into the affairs of to-day.

REDEMPTION, n. Deliverance of sinners from the penalty of their sin, through their murder of the deity against whom they sinned. The doctrine of Redemption is the fundamental mystery of our holy religion, and whoso believeth in it shall not perish, but have everlasting life in which to try to understand it.

> *We must awake Man's spirit from his sin,*
> *And take some special measure for redeeming it;*
> *Though hard indeed the task to get it in*
> *Among the angels any way but teaming it,*
> *Or purify it otherwise than steaming it.*
> *I'm awkward at Redemption —a beginner:*
> *My method is to crucify the sinner. —Golgo Brone*

RELIGION, n. A daughter of Hope and Fear, explaining to Ignorance the nature of the Unknowable.

REPRESENTATIVE, n. In national politics, a member of the Lower House in this world, and without discernible hope of promotion in the next.

REPUBLIC, n. A nation in which, the thing governing and the thing governed being the same, there is only a permitted authority to enforce an optional obedience. In a republic, the foundation of public order is the ever lessening habit of submission inherited from ancestors who, being truly governed, submitted because they had to. There are as many kinds of republics as there are graduations between the despotism whence they came and the anarchy whither they lead.

REVOLUTION, n. In politics, an abrupt change in the form of misgovernment. Specifically, in American history, the substitution of the rule of an Administration for that of a Ministry, whereby the welfare and happiness of the people were advanced a full half-inch. Revolutions are usually accompanied by a considerable effusion of blood, but are accounted worth it — this appraisement being made by beneficiaries whose blood had not the mischance to be shed. The French revolution is of incalculable value to the Socialist of to-day; when he pulls the string actuating its bones its gestures are inexpressibly terrifying to gory tyrants suspected of fomenting law and order.

SACRAMENT, n. A solemn religious ceremony to which several degrees of authority and significance are attached. Rome has seven sacraments, but the Protestant churches, being less prosperous, feel that they can afford only two, and these of inferior sanctity. Some of the smaller sects have no sacraments at all — for which mean economy they will indubitably be damned.

SACRED, adj. Dedicated to some religious purpose; having a divine character; inspiring solemn thoughts or emotions; as, the Dalai Lama of Thibet; the Moogum of M'bwango; the temple of Apes in Ceylon; the Cow in India; the Crocodile, the Cat and the Onion of ancient Egypt; the Mufti of Moosh; the hair of the dog that bit Noah, etc.

> *All things are either sacred or profane.*
> *The former to ecclesiasts bring gain;*
> *The latter to the devil appertain.* —Dumbo Omohundro

SATAN, n. One of the Creator's lamentable mistakes, repented in sashcloth and axes. Being instated as an archangel, Satan made himself multifariously objectionable and was finally expelled from Heaven. Halfway in his descent he paused, bent his head in thought a moment and at last went back. "There is one favor that I should like to ask," said he.

"Name it."
"Man, I understand, is about to be created. He will need laws."
"What, wretch! you his appointed adversary, charged from the dawn of eternity with hatred of his soul — you ask for the right to make his laws?"
"Pardon; what I have to ask is that he be permitted to make them himself."
It was so ordered.

SENATE, n. A body of elderly gentlemen charged with high duties and misdemeanors.

SUFFRAGE, n. Expression of opinion by means of a ballot. The right of suffrage (which is held to be both a privilege and a duty) means, as commonly interpreted, the right to vote for the man of another man's choice, and is highly prized. Refusal to do so has the bad name of "incivism." The incivilian, however, cannot be properly arraigned for his crime, for there is no legitimate accuser. If the accuser is himself guilty he has no standing in the court of opinion; if not, he profits by the crime, for A's abstention from voting gives greater weight to the vote of B. By female suffrage is meant the right of a woman to vote as some man tells her to. It is based on female responsibility, which is somewhat limited. The woman most eager to jump out of her petticoat to assert her rights is first to jump back into it when threatened with a switching for misusing them.

THEOSOPHY, n. An ancient faith having all the certitude of religion and all the mystery of science. The modern Theosophist holds, with the Buddhists, that we live an incalculable number of times on this earth, in as many several bodies, because one life is not long enough for our complete spiritual development; that is, a single lifetime does not suffice for us to become as wise and good as we choose to wish to become. To be absolutely wise and good —that is perfection; and the Theosophist is so keen-sighted as to have observed that everything desirous of improvement eventually attains perfection. Less competent observers are disposed to except cats, which seem neither wiser nor better than they were last year. The greatest and fattest of recent Theosophists was the late Madame Blavatsky, who had no cat.

TRUST, n. In American politics, a large corporation composed in greater part of thrifty working men, widows of small means, orphans in the care of guardians and the courts, with many similar malefactors and public enemies.

VOTE, n. The instrument and symbol of a freeman's power to make a fool of himself and a wreck of his country.

WORSHIP, n. Homo Creator's testimony to the sound construction and fine finish of Deus Creatus. A popular form of abjection, having an element of pride.

Love & Marriage

AFFIANCED, pp. Fitted with an ankle-ring for the ball-and-chain.

BRIDE, n. A woman with a fine prospect of happiness behind her.

FEMALE, n. One of the opposing, or unfair, sex.

> *The Maker, at Creation's birth,*
> *With living things had stocked the earth.*
> *From elephants to bats and snails,*
> *They all were good, for all were males.*
> *But when the Devil came and saw*
> *He said: "By Thine eternal law*
> *Of growth, maturity, decay,*
> *These all must quickly pass away*
> *And leave untenanted the earth*
> *Unless Thou dost establish birth" —*
> *Then tucked his head beneath his wing*
> *To laugh — he had no sleeve — the thing*
> *With deviltry did so accord,*
> *That he'd suggested to the Lord.*
> *The Master pondered this advice,*

Then shook and threw the fateful dice
Wherewith all matters here below
Are ordered, and observed the throw;
Then bent His head in awful state,
Confirming the decree of Fate.
From every part of earth anew
The conscious dust consenting flew,
While rivers from their courses rolled
To make it plastic for the mould.
Enough collected (but no more,
For niggard Nature hoards her store)
He kneaded it to flexible clay,
While Nick unseen threw some away.
And then the various forms He cast,
Gross organs first and finer last;
No one at once evolved, but all
By even touches grew and small
Degrees advanced, till, shade by shade,
To match all living things He'd made
Females, complete in all their parts
Except (His clay gave out) the hearts.
"No matter," Satan cried; "with speed
I'll fetch the very hearts they need" —
So flew away and soon brought back
The number needed, in a sack.
That night earth rang with sounds of strife —
Ten million males each had a wife;
That night sweet Peace her pinions spread
O'er Hell —ten million devils dead! —G.J.

HERS, pron. His.

HUSBAND, n. One who, having dined, is charged with the care of the plate.

INCOMPATIBILITY, n. In matrimony a similarity of tastes, particularly the taste for domination. Incompatibility may, however, consist of a meek-eyed matron living just around the corner. It has even been known to wear a moustache.

JEALOUS, adj. Unduly concerned about the preservation of that which can be lost only if not worth keeping.

KISS, n. A word invented by the poets as a rhyme for "bliss." It is supposed to signify, in a general way, some kind of rite or ceremony appertaining to a good understanding; but the manner of its performance is unknown to this lexicographer.

LOVE, n. A temporary insanity curable by marriage or by removal of the patient from the influences under which he incurred the disorder. This disease, like caries and many other ailments, is prevalent only among civilized races living under artificial conditions; barbarous nations breathing pure air and eating simple food enjoy immunity from its ravages. It is sometimes fatal, but more frequently to the physician than to the patient.

MAIDEN, n. A young person of the unfair sex addicted to clewless conduct and views that madden to crime. The genus has a wide geographical distribution, being found wherever sought and deplored wherever found. The maiden is not altogether unpleasing to the eye, nor (without her piano and her views) insupportable to the ear, though in respect to comeliness distinctly inferior to the rainbow, and, with regard to the part of her that is audible, beaten out of the field by the canary — which, also, is more portable.

MALE, n. A member of the unconsidered, or negligible sex. The male of the human race is commonly known (to the female) as Mere Man. The genus has two varieties: good providers and bad providers.

MARRIAGE, n. The state or condition of a community consisting of a master, a mistress and two slaves, making in all, two.

WEDDING, n. A ceremony at which two persons undertake to become one, one undertakes to become nothing, and nothing undertakes to become supportable.

Science & Philosophy

CARTESIAN, adj. Relating to Descartes, a famous philosopher, author of the celebrated dictum, Cogito ergo sum — whereby he was pleased to suppose he demonstrated the reality of human existence. The dictum might be improved, however, thus: Cogito cogito ergo cogito sum —"I think that I think, therefore I think that I am;" as close an approach to certainty as any philosopher has yet made.

CLAIRVOYANT, n. A person, commonly a woman, who has the power of seeing that which is invisible to her patron, namely, that he is a blockhead.

EGOTIST, n. A person of low taste, more interested in himself than in me.

> *Megaceph, chosen to serve the State*
> *In the halls of legislative debate,*
> *One day with all his credentials came*
> *To the capitol's door and announced his name.*
> *The doorkeeper looked, with a comical twist*
> *Of the face, at the eminent egotist,*
> *And said: "Go away, for we settle here*
> *All manner of questions, knotty and queer,*
> *And we cannot have, when the speaker demands*
> *To be told how every member stands,*
> *A man who to all things under the sky*
> *Assents by eternally voting 'I.'"*

ETHNOLOGY, n. The science that treats of the various tribes of Man, as robbers, thieves, swindlers, dunces, lunatics, idiots and ethnologists.

FAITH, n. Belief without evidence in what is told by one who speaks without knowledge, of things without parallel.

FASHION, n. A despot whom the wise ridicule and obey.

A king there was who lost an eye
In some excess of passion;
And straight his courtiers all did try
To follow the new fashion.

Each dropped one eyelid when before
The throne he ventured, thinking
Twould please the king. That monarch swore
He'd slay them all for winking.

What should they do? They were not hot
To hazard such disaster;
They dared not close an eye — dared not
See better than their master.

Seeing them lacrymose and glum,
A leech consoled the weepers:
He spread small rags with liquid gum
And covered half their peepers.

The court all wore the stuff, the flame
Of royal anger dying.
That's how court-plaster got its name
Unless I'm greatly lying. —Naramy Oof

GEOLOGY, n. The science of the earth's crust — to which, doubtless, will be added that of its interior whenever a man shall come up
garrulous out of a well. The geological formations of the globe
already noted are catalogued thus: The Primary, or lower one, consists of rocks, bones or mired mules, gas-pipes, miners' tools, antique
statues minus the nose, Spanish doubloons and ancestors. The
Secondary is largely made up of red worms and moles. The Tertiary

comprises railway tracks, patent pavements, grass, snakes, mouldy boots, beer bottles, tomato cans, intoxicated citizens, garbage, anarchists, snap-dogs and fools.

GRAVITATION, n. The tendency of all bodies to approach one another with a strength proportioned to the quantity of matter they contain — the quantity of matter they contain being ascertained by the strength of their tendency to approach one another. This is a lovely and edifying illustration of how science, having made A the proof of B, makes B the proof of A.

MAGNET, n. Something acted upon by magnetism.

MAGNETISM, n. Something acting upon a magnet.

MAGNITUDE, n. Size. Magnitude being purely relative, nothing is large and nothing small. If everything in the universe were increased in bulk one thousand diameters nothing would be any larger than it was before, but if one thing remained unchanged all the others would be larger than they had been. To an understanding familiar with the relativity of magnitude and distance the spaces and masses of the astronomer would be no more impressive than those of the microscopist. For anything we know to the contrary, the visible universe may be a small part of an atom, with its component ions, floating in the life-fluid (luminiferous ether) of some animal. Possibly the wee creatures peopling the corpuscles of our own blood are overcome with the proper emotion when contemplating the unthinkable distance from one of these to another.

MIND, n. A mysterious form of matter secreted by the brain. Its chief activity consists in the endeavor to ascertain its own nature, the futility of the attempt being due to the fact that it has nothing but itself to know itself with. From the Latin *mens*, a fact unknown to that honest shoe-seller, who, observing that his learned competitor over the way had displayed the motto *"Mens scia recti,"* emblazoned his own front with the words "Men's, women's and children's conscia recti."

MOLECULE, n. The ultimate, indivisible unit of matter. It is distinguished from the corpuscle, also the ultimate, indivisible unit of matter, by a closer resemblance to the atom, also the ultimate, indivisible unit of matter. Three great scientific theories of the structure of the universe are the molecular, the corpuscular and the atomic. A fourth affirms, with Haeckel, the condensation of precipitation of matter from ether — whose existence is proved by the condensation of precipitation. The present trend of scientific thought is toward the theory of ions. The ion differs from the molecule, the corpuscle and the atom in that it is an ion. A fifth theory is held by idiots, but it is doubtful if they know any more about the matter than the others.

MONAD, n. The ultimate, indivisible unit of matter. (See Molecule.) According to Leibnitz, as nearly as he seems willing to be understood, the monad has body without bulk, and mind without manifestation — Leibnitz knows him by the innate power of considering. He has founded upon him a theory of the universe, which the creature bears without resentment, for the monad is a gentleman. Small as he is, the monad contains all the powers and possibilities needful to his evolution into a German philosopher of the first class — altogether a very capable little fellow. He is not to be confounded with the microbe, or bacillus; by its inability to discern him, a good microscope shows him to be of an entirely distinct species.

NEWTONIAN, adj. Pertaining to a philosophy of the universe invented by Newton, who discovered that an apple will fall to the ground, but was unable to say why. His successors and disciples have advanced so far as to be able to say when.

NIHILIST, n. A Russian who denies the existence of anything but Tolstoi. The leader of the school is Tolstoi.

OBSERVATORY, n. A place where astronomers conjecture away the guesses of their predecessors.

PHILOSOPHY, n. A route of many roads leading from nowhere to nothing.

PLATONIC, adj. Pertaining to the philosophy of Socrates. Platonic Love is a fool's name for the affection between a disability and a frost.

RATIONAL, adj. Devoid of all delusions save those of observation, experience and reflection.

REALITY, n. The dream of a mad philosopher. That which would remain in the cupel if one should assay a phantom. The nucleus of a vacuum.

REALLY, adv. Apparently.

SELF-EVIDENT, adj. Evident to one's self and to nobody else.

TRUTH, n. An ingenious compound of desirability and appearance. Discovery of truth is the sole purpose of philosophy, which is the most ancient occupation of the human mind and has a fair prospect of existing with increasing activity to the end of time.

ZOOLOGY, n. The science and history of the animal kingdom, including its king, the House Fly *(Musca maledicta)*. The father of Zoology was Aristotle, as is universally conceded, but the name of its mother has not come down to us. Two of the science's most illustrious expounders were Buffon and Oliver Goldsmith, from both of whom we learn *(L'Histoire g én érale des animaux* and *A History of Animated Nature)* that the domestic cow sheds its horn every two years.

Language & Literature

ADAGE, n. Boned wisdom for weak teeth.

BLANK-VERSE, n. Unrhymed iambic pentameters — the most difficult kind of English verse to write acceptably; a kind, therefore, much affected by those who cannot acceptably write any kind.

DICTIONARY, n. A malevolent literary device for cramping the growth of a language and making it hard and inelastic. This dictionary, however, is a most useful work.

ELEGY, n. A composition in verse, in which, without employing any of the methods of humor, the writer aims to produce in the

reader's mind the dampest kind of dejection. The most famous
English example begins somewhat like this:

The cur foretells the knell of parting day;
The loafing herd winds slowly o'er the lea;
The wise man homeward plods; I only stay
To fiddle-faddle in a minor key.

EPIGRAM, n. A short, sharp saying in prose or verse, frequently
characterize by acidity or acerbity and sometimes by wisdom.
Following are some of the more notable epigrams of the learned
and ingenious Dr. Jamrach Holobom:

We know better the needs of ourselves than of others. To serve one-
self is economy of administration.

In each human heart are a tiger, a pig, an ass and a nightingale.
Diversity of character is due to their unequal activity.

There are three sexes; males, females and girls.

Beauty in women and distinction in men are alike in this: they
seem to the unthinking a kind of credibility.

Women in love are less ashamed than men. They have less to be
ashamed of.

While your friend holds you affectionately by both your hands you
are safe, for you can watch both his.

LANGUAGE, n. The music with which we charm the serpents
guarding another's treasure.

LEXICOGRAPHER, n. A pestilent fellow who, under the pretense
of recording some particular stage in the development of a language, does what he can to arrest its growth, stiffen its flexibility
and mechanize its methods. For your lexicographer, having written

his dictionary, comes to be considered "as one having authority," whereas his function is only to make a record, not to give a law. The natural servility of the human understanding having invested him with judicial power, surrenders its right of reason and submits itself to a chronicle as if it were a statute. Let the dictionary (for example) mark a good word as "obsolete" or "obsolescent" and few men thereafter venture to use it, whatever their need of it and however desirable its restoration to favor — whereby the process of improverishment is accelerated and speech decays. On the contrary, recognizing the truth that language must grow by innovation if it grow at all, makes new words and uses the old in an unfamiliar sense, has no following and is tartly reminded that "it isn't in the dictionary" — although down to the time of the first lexicographer (Heaven forgive him!) no author ever had used a word that was in the dictionary. In the golden prime and high noon of English speech; when from the lips of the great Elizabethans fell words that made their own meaning and carried it in their very sound; when a Shakespeare and a Bacon were possible, and the language now rapidly perishing at one end and slowly renewed at the other was in vigorous growth and hardy preservation — sweeter than honey and stronger than a lion — the lexicographer was a person unknown, the dictionary a creation which his Creator had not created him to create.

> *God said: "Let Spirit perish into Form,"*
> *And lexicographers arose, a swarm!*
> *Thought fled and left her clothing, which they took,*
> *And catalogued each garment in a book.*
> *Now, from her leafy covert when she cries:*
> *"Give me my clothes and I'll return," they rise*
> *And scan the list, and say without compassion:*
> *"Excuse us — they are mostly out of fashion." —Sigismund Smith*

MONOSYLLABIC, adj. Composed of words of one syllable, for literary babes who never tire of testifying their delight in the vapid compound by appropriate googoogling. The words are commonly Saxon — that is to say, words of a barbarous people destitute of ideas and incapable of any but the most elementary sentiments and emotions.

The man who writes in Saxon
Is the man to use an ax on. —*Judibras*

NOVEL, n. A short story padded. A species of composition bearing the same relation to literature that the panorama bears to art. As it is too long to be read at a sitting the impressions made by its successive parts are successively effaced, as in the panorama. Unity, totality of effect, is impossible; for besides the few pages last read all that is carried in mind is the mere plot of what has gone before. To the romance the novel is what photography is to painting. Its distinguishing principle, probability, corresponds to the literal actuality of the photograph and puts it distinctly into the category of reporting; whereas the free wing of the romancer enables him to mount to such altitudes of imagination as he may be fitted to attain; and the first three essentials of the literary art are imagination, imagination and imagination. The art of writing novels, such as it was, is long dead everywhere except in Russia, where it is new. Peace to its ashes — some of which have a large sale.

OBSOLETE, adj. No longer used by the timid. Said chiefly of words. A word which some lexicographer has marked obsolete is ever thereafter an object of dread and loathing to the fool writer, but if it is a good word and has no exact modern equivalent equally good, it is good enough for the good writer. Indeed, a writer's attitude toward "obsolete" words is as true a measure of his literary ability as anything except the character of his work. A dictionary of obsolete and obsolescent words would not only be singularly rich in strong and sweet parts of speech; it would add large possessions to the vocabulary of every competent writer who might not happen to be a competent reader.

ORTHOGRAPHY, n. The science of spelling by the eye instead of the ear. Advocated with more heat than light by the outmates of every asylum for the insane. They have had to concede a few things since the time of Chaucer, but are none the less hot in defence of those to be conceded hereafter.

A spelling reformer indicted
For fudge was before the court cicted.
The judge said: "Enough —
His candle we'll snough,
And his sepulchre shall not be whicted."

PLATITUDE, n. The fundamental element and special glory of popular literature. A thought that snores in words that smoke. The wisdom of a million fools in the diction of a dullard. A fossil sentiment in artificial rock. A moral without the fable. All that is mortal of a departed truth. A demi-tasse of milk-and-mortality. The Pope's-nose of a featherless peacock. A jelly-fish withering on the shore of the sea of thought. The cackle surviving the egg. A desiccated epigram.

POETRY, n. A form of expression peculiar to the Land beyond the Magazines.

REALISM, n. The art of depicting nature as it is seem by toads. The charm suffusing a landscape painted by a mole, or a story written by a measuring-worm.

RIME, n. Agreeing sounds in the terminals of verse, mostly bad. The verses themselves, as distinguished from prose, mostly dull. Usually (and wickedly) spelled "rhyme."

RIMER, n. A poet regarded with indifference or disesteem.

The rimer quenches his unheeded fires,
The sound surceases and the sense expires.
Then the domestic dog, to east and west,
Expounds the passions burning in his breast.
The rising moon o'er that enchanted land
Pauses to hear and yearns to understand. —Mowbray Myles

ROMANCE, n. Fiction that owes no allegiance to the God of Things as They Are. In the novel the writer's thought is tethered to probability, as a domestic horse to the hitching-post, but in romance it ranges at will over the entire region of the imagination — free, lawless, immune to bit and rein. Your novelist is a poor creature, as Carlyle might say — a mere reporter. He may invent his characters and plot, but he must not imagine anything taking place that might not occur, albeit his entire narrative is candidly a lie. Why he imposes this hard condition on himself, and "drags at each remove a lengthening chain" of his own forging he can explain in ten thick volumes without illuminating by so much as a candle's ray the black profound of his own ignorance of the matter. There are great novels, for great writers have "laid waste their powers" to write them, but it remains true that far and away the most fascinating fiction that we have is "The Thousand and One Nights."

SALACITY, n. A certain literary quality frequently observed in popular novels, especially in those written by women and young girls, who give it another name and think that in introducing it they are occupying a neglected field of letters and reaping an overlooked harvest. If they have the misfortune to live long enough they are tormented with a desire to burn their sheaves.

SATIRE, n. An obsolete kind of literary composition in which the vices and follies of the author's enemies were expounded with imperfect tenderness. In this country satire never had more than a sickly and uncertain existence, for the soul of it is wit, wherein we are dolefully deficient, the humor that we mistake for it, like all humor, being tolerant and sympathetic. Moreover, although Americans are "endowed by their Creator" with abundant vice and folly, it is not generally known that these are reprehensible qualities, wherefore the satirist is popularly regarded as a soul-spirited knave, and his every victim's outcry for codefendants evokes a national assent.

Hail Satire! be thy praises ever sung
In the dead language of a mummy's tongue,
For thou thyself art dead, and damned as well —

Thy spirit (usefully employed) in Hell.
Had it been such as consecrates the Bible
Thou hadst not perished by the law of libel. —Barney Stims

SAW, n. A trite popular saying, or proverb. (Figurative and colloqui-
al.) So called because it makes its way into a wooden head. Following
are examples of old saws fitted with new teeth.

A penny saved is a penny to squander.

A man is known by the company that he organizes.

A bad workman quarrels with the man who calls him that.

A bird in the hand is worth what it will bring.

Better late than before anybody has invited you.

Example is better than following it.

Half a loaf is better than a whole one if there is much else.

Think twice before you speak to a friend in need.

What is worth doing is worth the trouble of asking somebody to do it.

Least said is soonest disavowed.

He laughs best who laughs least.

Speak of the Devil and he will hear about it.

Of two evils choose to be the least.

Strike while your employer has a big contract.

Where there's a will there's a won't.

SCRIBBLER, n. A professional writer whose views are antagonistic to one's own.

SLANG, n. The grunt of the human hog *(Pignoramus intolerabilis)* with an audible memory. The speech of one who utters with his tongue what he thinks with his ear, and feels the pride of a creator in accomplishing the feat of a parrot. A means (under Providence) of setting up as a wit without a capital of sense.

TYPE, n. Pestilent bits of metal suspected of destroying civilization and enlightenment, despite their obvious agency in this incomparable dictionary.

USAGE, n. The First Person of the literary Trinity, the Second and Third being Custom and Conventionality. Imbued with a decent reverence for this Holy Triad an industrious writer may hope to produce books that will live as long as the fashion.

VITUPERATION, n. Satire, as understood by dunces and all such as suffer from an impediment in their wit.

WIT, n. The salt with which the American humorist spoils his intellectual cookery by leaving it out.

Morals & Manners

ABILITY, n. The natural equipment to accomplish some small part of the meaner ambitions distinguishing able men from dead ones. In the last analysis ability is commonly found to consist mainly in a high degree of solemnity. Perhaps, however, this impressive quality is rightly appraised; it is no easy task to be solemn.

ABNORMAL, adj. Not conforming to standard. In matters of thought and conduct, to be independent is to be abnormal, to be abnormal is to be detested. Wherefore the lexicographer adviseth a striving toward the straiter resemblance of the Average Man than he hath to himself. Whoso attaineth thereto shall have peace, the prospect of death and the hope of Hell.

ABSURDITY, n. A statement or belief manifestly inconsistent with one's own opinion.

ACCOUNTABILITY, n. The mother of caution.

"My accountability, bear in mind,"
Said the Grand Vizier: "Yes, yes,"
Said the Shah: "I do—'tis the only kind
Of ability you possess." —Joram Tate

ACHIEVEMENT, n. The death of endeavor and the birth of disgust.

ACQUAINTANCE, n. A person whom we know well enough to borrow from, but not well enough to lend to. A degree of friendship called slight when its object is poor or obscure, and intimate when he is rich or famous.

ALONE, adj. In bad company.

In contact, lo! the flint and steel,
By spark and flame, the thought reveal
That he the metal, she the stone,
Had cherished secretly alone. —Booley Fito

APPLAUSE, n. The echo of a platitude.

ARTLESSNESS, n. A certain engaging quality to which women attain by long study and severe practice upon the admiring male, who is pleased to fancy it resembles the candid simplicity of his young.

BACK, n. That part of your friend which it is your privilege to contemplate in your adversity.

BACKBITE, v.t. To speak of a man as you find him when he can't find you.

BAIT, n. A preparation that renders the hook more palatable. The best kind is beauty.

BEGGAR, n. One who has relied on the assistance of his friends.

BENEFACTOR, n. One who makes heavy purchases of ingratitude, without, however, materially affecting the price, which is still within the means of all.

BIGOT, n. One who is obstinately and zealously attached to an opinion that you do not entertain.

BIRTH, n. The first and direst of all disasters. As to the nature of it there appears to be no uniformity. Castor and Pollux were born from the egg. Pallas came out of a skull. Galatea was once a block of stone. Peresilis, who wrote in the tenth century, avers that he grew up out of the ground where a priest had spilled holy water. It is known that Arimaxus was derived from a hole in the earth, made by a stroke of lightning. Leucomedon was the son of a cavern in Mount Aetna, and I have myself seen a man come out of a wine cellar.

BORE, n. A person who talks when you wish him to listen.

CALAMITY, n. A more than commonly plain and unmistakable reminder that the affairs of this life are not of our own ordering. Calamities are of two kinds: misfortune to ourselves, and good fortune to others.

CALLOUS, adj. Gifted with great fortitude to bear the evils afflicting another.

CANNIBAL, n. A gastronome of the old school who preserves the simple tastes and adheres to the natural diet of the pre-pork period.

COMFORT, n. A state of mind produced by contemplation of a neighbor's uneasiness.

CONGRATULATION, n. The civility of envy.

CONSOLATION, n. The knowledge that a better man is more unfortunate than yourself.

CONSULT, v.i. To seek another's disapproval of a course already decided on.

CONTROVERSY, n. A battle in which spittle or ink replaces the injurious cannon-ball and the inconsiderate bayonet.

In controversy with the facile tongue —
That bloodless warfare of the old and young —
So seek your adversary to engage
That on himself he shall exhaust his rage,
And, like a snake that's fastened to the ground,
With his own fangs inflict the fatal wound.
You ask me how this miracle is done?
Adopt his own opinions, one by one,
And taunt him to refute them; in his wrath
He'll sweep them pitilessly from his path.
Advance then gently all you wish to prove,
Each proposition prefaced with, "As you've
So well remarked," or, "As you wisely say,
And I cannot dispute," or, "By the way,
This view of it which, better far expressed,
Runs through your argument." Then leave the rest
To him, secure that he'll perform his trust
And prove your views intelligent and just. —Conmore Apel Brune

COWARD, n. One who in a perilous emergency thinks with his legs.

CREDITOR, n. One of a tribe of savages dwelling beyond the Financial Straits and dreaded for their desolating incursions.

CRITIC, n. A person who boasts himself hard to please because nobody tries to please him.

There is a land of pure delight,
Beyond the Jordan's flood,
Where saints, apparelled all in white,
Fling back the critic's mud.
And as he legs it through the skies,
His pelt a sable hue,
He sorrows sore to recognize
The missiles that he threw. —Orrin Goof

CURIOSITY, n. An objectionable quality of the female mind. The desire to know whether or not a woman is cursed with curiosity is one of the most active and insatiable passions of the masculine soul.

DAY, n. A period of twenty-four hours, mostly misspent. This period is divided into two parts, the day proper and the night, or day improper — the former devoted to sins of business, the latter consecrated to the other sort. These two kinds of social activity overlap.

DEBAUCHEE, n. One who has so earnestly pursued pleasure that he has had the misfortune to overtake it.

DEBT, n. An ingenious substitute for the chain and whip of the slave-driver.

> *As, pent in an aquarium, the troutlet*
> *Swims round and round his tank to find an outlet,*
> *Pressing his nose against the glass that holds him,*
> *Nor ever sees the prison that enfolds him;*
> *So the poor debtor, seeing naught around him,*
> *Yet feels the narrow limits that impound him,*
> *Grieves at his debt and studies to evade it,*
> *And finds at last he might as well have paid it. —Barlow S. Vode*

DEFENCELESS, adj. Unable to attack.

DELIBERATION, n. The act of examining one's bread to determine which side it is buttered on.

DESTINY, n. A tyrant's authority for crime and a fool's excuse for failure.

DISCRIMINATE, v.i. To note the particulars in which one person or thing is, if possible, more objectionable than another.

DISCUSSION, n. A method of confirming others in their errors.

DISOBEDIENCE, n. The silver lining to the cloud of servitude.

DULLARD, n. A member of the reigning dynasty in letters and

life. The Dullards came in with Adam, and being both numerous and sturdy have overrun the habitable world. The secret of their power is their insensibility to blows; tickle them with a bludgeon and they laugh with a platitude. The Dullards came originally from Boeotia, whence they were driven by stress of starvation, their dullness having blighted the crops. For some centuries they infested Philistia, and many of them are called Philistines to this day. In the turbulent times of the Crusades they withdrew thence and gradually overspread all Europe, occupying most of the high places in politics, art, literature, science and theology. Since a detachment of Dullards came over with the Pilgrims in the *Mayflower* and made a favorable report of the country, their increase by birth, immigration, and conversion has been rapid and steady. According to the most trustworthy statistics the number of adult Dullards in the United States is but little short of thirty millions, including the statisticians. The intellectual centre of the race is somewhere about Peoria, Illinois, but the New England Dullard is the most shockingly moral.

ECCENTRICITY, n. A method of distinction so cheap that fools employ it to accentuate their incapacity.

EDUCATION, n. That which discloses to the wise and disguises from the foolish their lack of understanding.

ENVY, n. Emulation adapted to the meanest capacity.

ERUDITION, n. Dust shaken out of a book into an empty skull.

EULOGY, n. Praise of a person who has either the advantages of wealth and power, or the consideration to be dead.

EXCESS, n. In morals, an indulgence that enforces by appropriate penalties the law of moderation.

> *Hail, high Excess — especially in wine,*
> *To thee in worship do I bend the knee*
> *Who preach abstemiousness unto me —*
> *My skull thy pulpit, as my paunch thy shrine.*
> *Precept on precept, aye, and line on line,*

Could ne'er persuade so sweetly to agree
With reason as thy touch, exact and free,
Upon my forehead and along my spine.
At thy command eschewing pleasure's cup,
With the hot grape I warm no more my wit;
When on thy stool of penitence I sit
I'm quite converted, for I can't get up.
Ungrateful he who afterward would falter
To make new sacrifices at thine altar!

EXPERIENCE, n. The wisdom that enables us to recognize as an undesirable old acquaintance the folly that we have already embraced.

FIDELITY, n. A virtue peculiar to those who are about to be betrayed.

FRIENDLESS, adj. Having no favors to bestow. Destitute of fortune. Addicted to utterance of truth and common sense.

FRIENDSHIP, n. A ship big enough to carry two in fair weather, but only one in foul.

GLUTTON, n. A person who escapes the evils of moderation by committing dyspepsia.

GOOD, adj. Sensible, madam, to the worth of this present writer. Alive, sir, to the advantages of letting him alone.

HABIT, n. A shackle for the free.

HAPPINESS, n. An agreeable sensation arising from contemplating the misery of another.

HEAVEN, n. A place where the wicked cease from troubling you with talk of their personal affairs, and the good listen with attention while you expound your own.

HONORABLE, adj. Afflicted with an impediment in one's reach. In legislative bodies it is customary to mention all members as honorable; as, "the honorable gentleman is a scurvy cur."

HOPE, n. Desire and expectation rolled into one.

> *Delicious Hope! when naught to man it left —*
> *Of fortune destitute, of friends bereft;*
> *When even his dog deserts him, and his goat*
> *With tranquil disaffection chews his coat*
> *While yet it hangs upon his back; then thou,*
> *The star far-flaming on thine angel brow,*
> *Descendest, radiant, from the skies to hint*
> *The promise of a clerkship in the Mint. —Fogarty Weffing*

HOSPITALITY, n. The virtue which induces us to feed and lodge certain persons who are not in need of food and lodging.

HYPOCRITE, n. One who, professing virtues that he does not respect, secures the advantage of seeming to be what he depises.

ICONOCLAST, n. A breaker of idols, the worshipers whereof are imperfectly gratified by the performance, and most strenuously protest that he unbuildeth but doth not reëdify, that he pulleth down but pileth not up. For the poor things would have other idols in place of those he thwacketh upon the mazzard and dispelleth. But the iconoclast saith: "Ye shall have none at all, for ye need them not; and if the rebuilder fooleth round hereabout, behold I will depress the head of him and sit thereon till he squawk it."

IDLENESS, n. A model farm where the devil experiments with seeds of new sins and promotes the growth of staple vices.

IGNORAMUS, n. A person unacquainted with certain kinds of knowledge familiar to yourself, and having certain other kinds that you know nothing about.

> *Dumble was an ignoramus,*
> *Mumble was for learning famous.*
> *Mumble said one day to Dumble:*
> *"Ignorance should be more humble.*
> *Not a spark have you of knowledge*
> *That was got in any college."*

Dumble said to Mumble: "Truly
You're self-satisfied unduly.
Of things in college I'm denied
A knowledge — you of all beside." —Borelli

IMMORAL, adj. Inexpedient. Whatever in the long run and with regard to the greater number of instances men find to be generally inexpedient comes to be considered wrong, wicked, immoral. If man's notions of right and wrong have any other basis than this of expediency; if they originated, or could have originated, in any other way; if actions have in themselves a moral character apart from, and nowise dependent on, their consequences — then all philosophy is a lie and reason a disorder of the mind.

IMPROVIDENCE, n. Provision for the needs of to-day from the revenues of to-morrow.

IMPUNITY, n. Wealth.

INJURY, n. An offense next in degree of enormity to a slight.

INJUSTICE, n. A burden which of all those that we load upon others and carry ourselves is lightest in the hands and heaviest upon the back.

LAZINESS, n. Unwarranted repose of manner in a person of low degree.

LEARNING, n. The kind of ignorance distinguishing the studious.

LIFE, n. A spiritual pickle preserving the body from decay. We live in daily apprehension of its loss; yet when lost it is not missed. The question, "Is life worth living?" has been much discussed; particularly by those who think it is not, many of whom have written at great length in support of their view and by careful observance of the laws of health enjoyed for long terms of years the honors of successful controversy.

"Life's not worth living, and that's the truth,"
Carelessly caroled the golden youth.

In manhood still he maintained that view
And held it more strongly the older he grew.
When kicked by a jackass at eighty-three,
"Go fetch me a surgeon at once!" cried he. —Han Soper

MAD, adj. Affected with a high degree of intellectual independence; not conforming to standards of thought, speech and action derived by the conformants from study of themselves; at odds with the majority; in short, unusual. It is noteworthy that persons are pronounced mad by officials destitute of evidence that themselves are sane. For illustration, this present (and illustrious) lexicographer is no firmer in the faith of his own sanity than is any inmate of any madhouse in the land; yet for aught he knows to the contrary, instead of the lofty occupation that seems to him to be engaging his powers he may really be beating his hands against the window bars of an asylum and declaring himself Noah Webster, to the innocent delight of many thoughtless spectators.

ME, pro. The objectionable case of I. The personal pronoun in English has three cases, the dominative, the objectionable and the oppressive. Each is all three.

MENDACIOUS, adj. Addicted to rhetoric.

MERCY, n. An attribute beloved of detected offenders.

OUTDO, v.t. To make an enemy.

PATIENCE, n. A minor form of despair, disguised as a virtue.

PIANO, n. A parlor utensil for subduing the impenitent visitor. It is operated by depressing the keys of the machine and the spirits of the audience.

PLUNDER, v. To take the property of another without observing the decent and customary reticences of theft. To effect a change of ownership with the candid concomitance of a brass band. To wrest the wealth of A from B and leave C lamenting a vanishing opportunity.

POCKET, n. The cradle of motive and the grave of conscience. In woman this organ is lacking; so she acts without motive, and her conscience, denied burial, remains ever alive, confessing the sins of others.

PRESENT, n. That part of eternity dividing the domain of disappointment from the realm of hope.

QUILL, n. An implement of torture yielded by a goose and commonly wielded by an ass. This use of the quill is now obsolete, but its modern equivalent, the steel pen, is wielded by the same everlasting Presence.

RAILROAD, n. The chief of many mechanical devices enabling us to get away from where we are to where we are no better off. For this purpose the railroad is held in highest favor by the optimist, for it permits him to make the transit with great expedition.

REASON, v.i. To weigh probabilities in the scales of desire.

REASON, n. Propensitate of prejudice.

REPARATION, n. Satisfaction that is made for a wrong and deducted from the satisfaction felt in committing it.

REPARTEE, n. Prudent insult in retort. Practiced by gentlemen with a constitutional aversion to violence, but a strong disposition to offend. In a war of words, the tactics of the North American Indian.

RESOLUTE, adj. Obstinate in a course that we approve.

RESPECTABILITY, n. The offspring of a liaison between a bald head and a bank account.

RESPONSIBILITY, n. A detachable burden easily shifted to the shoulders of God, Fate, Fortune, Luck or one's neighbor. In the days of astrology it was customary to unload it upon a star.

Alas, things ain't what we should see
If Eve had let that apple be;
And many a feller which had ought
To set with monarchses of thought,

Or play some rosy little game
With battle-chaps on fields of fame,
Is downed by his unlucky star
And hollers: "Peanuts! — here you are!" — *"The Sturdy Beggar"*

SELFISH, adj. Devoid of consideration for the selfishness of others.

SYCOPHANT, n. One who approaches Greatness on his belly so that he may not be commanded to turn and be kicked. He is sometimes an editor.

TALK, v.t. To commit an indiscretion without temptation, from an impulse without purpose.

TEDIUM, n. Ennui, the state or condition of one that is bored. Many fanciful derivations of the word have been affirmed, but so high an authority as Father Jape says that it comes from a very obvious source — the first words of the ancient Latin hymn *Te Deum Laudamus*. In this apparently natural derivation there is something that saddens.

TELEPHONE, n. An invention of the devil which abrogates some of the advantages of making a disagreeable person keep his distance.

TWICE, adv. Once too often.

ZEAL, n. A certain nervous disorder afflicting the young and inexperienced. A passion that goeth before a sprawl.

Essays and Journalism

Much to the later annoyance and inconvenience of his scholars, Bierce declined to make room in his *Collected Works* for his journalism, particularly his popular feature columns of invective, which he disparaged as a lowly and unworthy form of writing. Yet many of the pieces he did collect—the stories, the polished essays, the entries to *The Devil's Dictionary*, the satiric verse—had their origins in his newspaper writing, first published in such evanescent venues as the *San Francisco News Letter*, the *Wasp*, and the *San Francisco Examiner*. No offense to Bierce, but the man was first and last a journalist, so that the title of this section is almost unavoidably redundant.

What I Saw of Shiloh

I

This is a simple story of a battle; such a tale as may be told by a soldier who is no writer to a reader who is no soldier.

The morning of Sunday, the sixth day of April, 1862, was bright and warm. Reveille had been sounded rather late, for the troops, wearied with long marching, were to have a day of rest. The men were idling about the embers of their bivouac fires; some preparing breakfast, others looking carelessly to the condition of their arms and accoutrements, against the inevitable inspection; still others were chatting with indolent dogmatism on that never-failing theme, the end and object of the campaign. Sentinels paced up and down the confused front with a lounging freedom of mien and stride that would not have been tolerated at another time. A few of them limped unsoldierly in deference to blistered feet. At a little distance in rear of the stacked arms were a few tents out of which frowsy-headed officers occasionally peered, languidly calling to their servants to fetch a basin of water, dust a coat or polish a scabbard. Trim young mounted orderlies, bearing dispatches obviously unimportant, urged their lazy nags by devious ways amongst the men, enduring with unconcern their good-humored raillery, the penalty of superior station. Little negroes of not very clearly defined status and function lolled on their stomachs, kicking their long, bare heels in the sunshine, or slumbered peacefully, unaware of the practical waggery prepared by white hands for their undoing.

Presently the flag hanging limp and lifeless at headquarters was seen to lift itself spiritedly from the staff. At the same instant was heard a dull, distant sound like the heavy breathing of some great animal below the horizon. The flag had lifted its head to listen. There was a momentary lull in the hum of the human swarm; then, as the flag drooped the hush passed away. But there were some hundreds more men on their feet than before; some thousands of hearts beating with a quicker pulse.

Again the flag made a warning sign, and again the breeze bore to our ears the long, deep sighing of iron lungs. The division, as if it had received the sharp word of command, sprang to its feet, and stood in groups at "attention." Even the little blacks got up. I have since seen similar effects produced by earthquakes; I am not sure but the ground was trembling then. The mess-cooks, wise in their generation, lifted the steaming camp-kettles off the fire and stood by to cast out. The mounted orderlies had somehow disappeared. Officers came ducking from beneath their tents and gathered in groups. Headquarters had become a swarming hive.

The sound of the great guns now came in regular throbbings— the strong, full pulse of the fever of battle. The flag flapped excitedly, shaking out its blazonry of stars and stripes with a sort of fierce delight. Toward the knot of officers in its shadow dashed from somewhere—he seemed to have burst out of the ground in a cloud of dust—a mounted aide-de-camp, and on the instant rose the sharp, clear notes of a bugle, caught up and repeated, and passed on by other bugles, until the level reaches of brown fields, the line of woods trending away to far hills, and the unseen valleys beyond were "telling of the sound," the farther, fainter strains half drowned in ringing cheers as the men ran to range themselves behind the stacks of arms. For this call was not the wearisome "general" before which the tents go down; it was the exhilarating "assembly," which goes to the heart as wine and stirs the blood like the kisses of a beautiful woman. Who that has heard it calling to him above the grumble of great guns can forget the wild intoxication of its music?

II

The Confederate forces in Kentucky and Tennessee had suffered a series of reverses, culminating in the loss of Nashville. The blow was severe: immense quantities of war material had fallen to the victor, together with all the important strategic points. General Johnston withdrew Beauregard's army to Corinth, in northern Mississippi, where he hoped so to recruit and equip it as to enable it to assume the offensive and retake the lost territory.

The town of Corinth was a wretched place—the capital of a swamp. It is a two days' march west of the Tennessee River, which here and for a hundred and fifty miles farther, to where it falls into the Ohio at Paducah, runs nearly north. It is navigable to this point—that is to say, to Pittsburg Landing, where Corinth got to it by a road worn through a thickly wooded country seamed with ravines and bayous, rising nobody knows where and running into the river under sylvan arches heavily draped with Spanish moss. In some places they were obstructed by fallen trees. The Corinth road was at certain seasons a branch of the Tennessee River. Its mouth was Pittsburg Landing. Here in 1862 were some fields and a house or two; now there are a national cemetery and other improvements.

It was at Pittsburg Landing that Grant established his army, with a river in his rear and two toy steamboats as a means of communication with the east side, whither General Buell with thirty thousand men was moving from Nashville to join him. The question has been asked, Why did General Grant occupy the enemy's side of the river in the face of a superior force before the arrival of Buell? Buell had a long way to come; perhaps Grant was weary of waiting. Certainly Johnston was, for in the gray of the morning of April 6th, when Buell's leading division was *en bivouac* near the little town of Savannah, eight or ten miles below, the Confederate forces, having moved out of Corinth two days before, fell upon Grant's advance brigades and destroyed them. Grant was at Savannah, but hastened to the Landing in time to find his camps in the hands of the enemy and the remnants of his beaten army cooped up with an impassable river at their backs for moral support. I have related how the news of this affair came to us at Savannah. It came on the wind—a messenger that does not bear copious details.

III

On the side of the Tennessee River, over against Pittsburg Landing, are some low bare hills, partly enclosed by a forest. In the dusk of the evening of April 6 this open space, as seen from the other side of the stream—whence, indeed, it was anxiously watched by thousands of eyes, to many of which it grew dark long before the sun went down—would have appeared to have been ruled in long, dark lines, with new lines being constantly drawn across. These lines were the regiments of Buell's leading division, which having moved up from Savannah through a country presenting nothing but interminable swamps and pathless "bottom lands," with rank overgrowths of jungle, was arriving at the scene of action breathless, footsore and faint with hunger. It had been a terrible race; some regiments had lost a third of their number from fatigue, the men dropping from the ranks as if shot, and left to recover or die at their leisure. Nor was the scene to which they had been invited likely to inspire the moral confidence that medicines physical fatigue. True, the air was full of thunder and the earth was trembling beneath their feet; and if there is truth in the theory of the conversion of force, these men were storing up energy from every shock that burst its waves upon their bodies. Perhaps this theory may better than another explain the tremendous endurance of men in battle. But the eyes reported only matter for despair.

Before us ran the turbulent river, vexed with plunging shells and obscured in spots by blue sheets of low-lying smoke. The two little steamers were doing their duty well. They came over to us empty and went back crowded, sitting very low in the water, apparently on the point of capsizing. The farther edge of the water could not be seen; the boats came out of the obscurity, took on their passengers and vanished in the darkness. But on the heights above, the battle was burning brightly enough; a thousand lights kindled and expired in every second of time. There were broad flushings in the sky, against which the branches of the trees showed black. Sudden flames burst out here and there, singly and in dozens. Fleeting streaks of fire crossed over to us by way of welcome. These expired in blinding flashes and fierce little rolls of smoke, attended with the peculiar metallic ring of bursting shells, and followed by the

musical humming of the fragments as they struck into the ground
on every side, making us wince, but doing little harm. The air was
full of noises. To the right and the left the musketry rattled smartly and petulantly; directly in front it sighed and growled. To the
experienced ear this meant that the death-line was an arc of which
the river was the chord. There were deep, shaking explosions and
smart shocks; the whisper of stray bullets and the hurtle of conical
shells; the rush of round shot. There were faint, desultory cheers,
such as announce a momentary or partial triumph. Occasionally,
against the glare behind the trees, could be seen moving black figures, singularly distinct but apparently no longer than a thumb.
They seemed to me ludicrously like the figures of demons in old
allegorical prints of hell. To destroy these and all their belongings
the enemy needed but another hour of daylight; the steamers in
that case would have been doing him fine service by bringing more
fish to his net. Those of us who had the good fortune to arrive late
could then have eaten our teeth in impotent rage. Nay, to make his
victory sure it did not need that the sun should pause in the heavens; one of the many random shots falling into the river would
have done the business had chance directed it into the engine-room
of a steamer. You can perhaps fancy the anxiety with which we
watched them leaping down.

But we had two other allies besides the night. Just where the
enemy had pushed his right flank to the river was the mouth of a
wide bayou, and here two gunboats had taken station. They too
were of the toy sort, plated perhaps with railway metals, perhaps
with boiler-iron. They staggered under a heavy gun or two each.
The bayou made an opening in the high bank of the river. The bank
was a parapet, behind which the gunboats crouched, firing up the
bayou as through an embrasure. The enemy was at this disadvantage: he could not get at the gunboats, and he could advance only by
exposing his flank to their ponderous missiles, one of which would
have broken a half-mile of his bones and made nothing of it. Very
annoying this must have been—these twenty gunners beating back
an army because a sluggish creek had been pleased to fall into a
river at one point rather than another. Such is the part that accident
may play in the game of war.

As a spectacle this was rather fine. We could just discern the black bodies of these boats, looking very much like turtles. But when they let off their big guns there was a conflagration. The river shuddered in its banks, and hurried on, bloody, wounded, terrified! Objects a mile away sprang toward our eyes as a snake strikes at the face of its victim. The report stung us to the brain, but we blessed it audibly. Then we could hear the great shell tearing away through the air until the sound died out in the distance; then, a surprisingly long time afterward, a dull, distant explosion and a sudden silence of small-arms told their own tale.

IV

There was, I remember, no elephant on the boat that passed us across that evening, nor, I think, any hippopotamus. These would have been out of place. We had, however, a woman. Whether the baby was somewhere on board I did not learn. She was a fine creature, this woman; somebody's wife. Her mission, as she understood it, was to inspire the failing heart with courage; and when she selected mine I felt less flattered by her preference than astonished by her penetration. How did she learn? She stood on the upper deck with the red blaze of battle bathing her beautiful face, the twinkle of a thousand rifles mirrored in her eyes; and displaying a small ivory-handled pistol, she told me in a sentence punctuated by the thunder of great guns that if it came to the worst she would do her duty like a man! I am proud to remember that I took off my hat to this little fool.

V

Along the sheltered strip of beach between the river bank and the water was a confused mass of humanity—several thousands of men. They were mostly unarmed; many were wounded; some dead. All the camp-following tribes were there; all the cowards; a few officers. Not one of them knew where his regiment was, nor if he had a regiment. Many had not. These men were defeated, beaten,

cowed. They were deaf to duty and dead to shame. A more demented crew never drifted to the rear of broken battalions. They would
have stood in their tracks and been shot down to a man by a
provost-marshal's guard, but they could not have been urged up
that bank. An army's bravest men are its cowards. The death which
they would not meet at the hands of the enemy they will meet at
the hands of their officers, with never a flinching.

Whenever a steamboat would land, this abominable mob had to
be kept off her with bayonets; when she pulled away, they sprang on
her and were pushed by scores into the water, where they were suffered to drown one another in their own way. The men disembark-
ing insulted them, shoved them, struck them. In return they
expressed their unholy delight in the certainty of our destruction
by the enemy.

By the time my regiment had reached the plateau night had put
an end to the struggle. A sputter of rifles would break out now and
then, followed perhaps by a spiritless hurrah. Occasionally a shell
from a far-away battery would come pitching down somewhere
near, with a whir crescendo, or flit above our heads with a whisper
like that made by the wings of a night bird, to smother itself in the
river. But there was no more fighting. The gunboats, however,
blazed away at set intervals all night long, just to make the enemy
uncomfortable and break him of his rest.

For us there was no rest. Foot by foot we moved through the
dusky fields, we knew not whither. There were men all about us,
but no camp-fires; to have made a blaze would have been madness.
The men were of strange regiments; they mentioned the names of
unknown generals. They gathered in groups by the wayside, asking
eagerly our numbers. They recounted the depressing incidents of
the day. A thoughtful officer shut their mouths with a sharp word
as he passed; a wise one coming after encouraged them to repeat
their doleful tale all along the line.

Hidden in hollows and behind clumps of rank brambles were
large tents, dimly lighted with candles, but looking comfortable.
The kind of comfort they supplied was indicated by pairs of men
entering and reappearing, bearing litters; by low moans from within and by long rows of dead with covered faces outside. These tents

were constantly receiving the wounded, yet were never full; they were continually ejecting the dead, yet were never empty. It was as if the helpless had been carried in and murdered, that they might not hamper those whose business it was to fall to-morrow.

The night was now black-dark; as is usual after a battle, it had begun to rain. Still we moved; we were being put into position by somebody. Inch by inch we crept along, treading on one another's heels by way of keeping together. Commands were passed along the line in whispers; more commonly none were given. When the men had pressed so closely together that they could advance no farther they stood stock-still, sheltering the locks of their rifles with their ponchos. In this position many fell asleep. When those in front suddenly stepped away those in the rear, roused by the tramping, hastened after with such zeal that the line was soon choked again. Evidently the head of the division was being piloted at a snail's pace by some one who did not feel sure of his ground. Very often we struck our feet against the dead; more frequently against those who still had spirit enough to resent it with a moan. These were lifted carefully to one side and abandoned. Some had sense enough to ask in their weak way for water. Absurd! Their clothes were soaken, their hair dank; their white faces, dimly discernible, were clammy and cold. Besides, none of us had any water. There was plenty coming, though, for before midnight a thunderstorm broke upon us with great violence. The rain, which had for hours been a dull drizzle, fell with a copiousness that stifled us; we moved in running water up to our ankles. Happily, we were in a forest of great trees heavily "decorated" with Spanish moss, or with an enemy standing to his guns the disclosures of the lightning might have been inconvenient. As it was, the incessant blaze enabled us to consult our watches and encouraged us by displaying our numbers; our black, sinuous line, creeping like a giant serpent beneath the trees, was apparently interminable. I am almost ashamed to say how sweet I found the companionship of those coarse men.

So the long night wore away, and as the glimmer of morning crept in through the forest we found ourselves in a more open country. But where? Not a sign of battle was here. The trees were neither splintered nor scarred, the underbrush was unmown, the

ground had no footprints but our own. It was as if we had broken
into glades sacred to eternal silence. I should not have been surprised to see sleek leopards come fawning about our feet, and milk-
white deer confront us with human eyes.

A few inaudible commands from an invisible leader had placed
us in order of battle. But where was the enemy? Where, too, were
the riddled regiments that we had come to save? Had our other
divisions arrived during the night and passed the river to assist us?
or were we to oppose our paltry five thousand breasts to an army
flushed with victory? What protected our right? Who lay upon
our left? Was there really anything in our front?

There came, borne to us on the raw morning air, the long, weird
note of a bugle. It was directly before us. It rose with a low, clear,
deliberate warble, and seemed to float in the gray sky like the note
of a lark. The bugle calls of the Federal and the Confederate armies
were the same: it was the "assembly"! As it died away I observed
that the atmosphere had suffered a change; despite the equilibrium
established by the storm, it was electric. Wings were growing on
blistered feet. Bruised muscles and jolted bones, shoulders pound-
ed by the cruel knapsack, eyelids leaden from lack of sleep—all
were pervaded by the subtle fluid, all were unconscious of their
clay. The men thrust forward their heads, expanded their eyes and
clenched their teeth. They breathed hard, as if throttled by tugging
at the leash. If you had laid your hand in the beard or hair of one
of these men it would have crackled and shot sparks.

VI

I suppose the country lying between Corinth and Pittsburg
Landing could boast a few inhabitants other than alligators. What
manner of people they were it is impossible to say, inasmuch as the
fighting dispersed, or possibly exterminated them; perhaps in
merely classing them as non-saurian I shall describe them with
sufficient particularity and at the same time avert from myself the
natural suspicion attaching to a writer who points out to persons
who do not know him the peculiarities of persons whom he does
not know. One thing, however, I hope I may without offense affirm

of these swamp-dwellers—they were pious. To what deity their
veneration was given—whether, like the Egyptians, they worshiped
the crocodile, or, like other Americans, adored themselves, I do not
presume to guess. But whoever, or whatever, may have been the
divinity whose ends they shaped, unto Him, or It, they had builded
a temple. This humble edifice, centrally situated in the heart of a
solitude, and conveniently accessible to the supersylvan crow, had
been christened Shiloh Chapel, whence the name of the battle. The
fact of a Christian church—assuming it to have been a Christian
church—giving name to a wholesale cutting of Christian throats by
Christian hands need not be dwelt on here; the frequency of its
recurrence in the history of our species has somewhat abated the
moral interest that would otherwise attach to it.

VII

Owing to the darkness, the storm and the absence of a road, it had
been impossible to move the artillery from the open ground about
the Landing. The privation was much greater in a moral than in a
material sense. The infantry soldier feels a confidence in this cum-
brous arm quite unwarranted by its actual achievements in thin-
ning out the opposition. There is something that inspires confidence in the way a gun dashes up to the front, shoving fifty or a
hundred men to one side as if it said, "Permit *me!*" Then it squares
its shoulders, calmly dislocates a joint in its back, sends away its
twenty-four legs and settles down with a quiet rattle which says as
plainly as possible, "I've come to stay." There is a superb scorn in its
grimly defiant attitude, with its nose in the air; it appears not so
much to threaten the enemy as deride him.

Our batteries were probably toiling after us somewhere; we
could only hope the enemy might delay his attack until they
should arrive. "He may delay his defense if he like," said a senten-
tious young officer to whom I had imparted this natural wish. He
had read the signs aright; the words were hardly spoken when a
group of staff officers about the brigade commander shot away in
divergent lines as if scattered by a whirlwind, and galloping each
to the commander of a regiment gave the word. There was a

momentary confusion of tongues, a thin line of skirmishers detached itself from the compact front and pushed forward, followed by its diminutive reserves of half a company each—one of which platoons it was my fortune to command. When the straggling line of skirmishers had swept four or five hundred yards ahead, "See," said one of my comrades, "she moves!" She did indeed, and in fine style, her front as straight as a string, her reserve regiments in columns doubled on the center, following in true subordination; no braying of brass to apprise the enemy, no fifing and drumming to amuse him; no ostentation of gaudy flags; no nonsense. This was a matter of business.

In a few moments we had passed out of the singular oasis that had so marvelously escaped the desolation of battle, and now the evidences of the previous day's struggle were present in profusion. The ground was tolerably level here, the forest less dense, mostly clear of undergrowth, and occasionally opening out into small natural meadows. Here and there were small pools—mere discs of rainwater with a tinge of blood. Riven and torn with cannon-shot, the trunks of the trees protruded bunches of splinters like hands, the fingers above the wound interlacing with those below. Large branches had been lopped, and hung their green heads to the ground, or swung critically in their netting of vines, as in a hammock. Many had been cut clean off and their masses of foliage seriously impeded the progress of the troops. The bark of these trees, from the root upward to a height of ten or twenty feet, was so thickly pierced with bullets and grape that one could not have laid a hand on it without covering several punctures. None had escaped. How the human body survives a storm like this must be explained by the fact that it is exposed to it but a few moments at a time, whereas these grand old trees had had no one to take their places, from the rising to the going down of the sun. Angular bits of iron, concavo-convex, sticking in the sides of muddy depressions, showed where shells had exploded in their furrows. Knapsacks, canteens, haversacks distended with soaken and swollen biscuits, gaping to disgorge, blankets beaten into the soil by the rain, rifles with bent barrels or splintered stocks, waist-belts, hats and the omnipresent sardine-box—all the wretched débris of the battle still littered the spongy earth as far as one could see, in every direction. Dead horses were everywhere; a few disabled caissons, or limbers, reclining on one elbow, as it were; ammunition wagons standing disconsolate behind four or six sprawling mules. Men? There were men enough; all dead, apparently, except one, who lay near where I had halted my platoon to await the slower movement of the line—a Federal sergeant, variously hurt, who had been a fine giant in his time. He lay face upward, taking in his breath in convulsive, rattling snorts, and blowing it out in sputters of froth which crawled creamily down his cheeks, piling itself alongside his neck and ears. A bullet had clipped a groove in his skull, above the temple; from this the brain protruded in bosses, dropping off in flakes and strings. I had not previously known one could get on, even in this unsatisfactory fashion, with so little brain. One of my men, whom I knew for a womanish fellow, asked if he should put his bayonet through him. Inexpressibly shocked by the cold-blooded proposal, I told him I thought not; it was unusual, and too many were looking.

VIII

It was plain that the enemy had retreated to Corinth. The arrival of our fresh troops and their successful passage of the river had disheartened him. Three or four of his gray cavalry videttes moving amongst the trees on the crest of a hill in our front, and galloping out of sight at the crack of our skirmishers' rifles, confirmed us in the belief; an army face to face with its enemy does not employ cavalry to watch its front. True, they might be a general and his staff. Crowning this rise we found a level field, a quarter of a mile in width; beyond it a gentle acclivity, covered with an undergrowth of young oaks, impervious to sight. We pushed on into the open, but the division halted at the edge. Having orders to conform to its movements, we halted too; but that did not suit; we received an intimation to proceed. I had performed this sort of service before, and in the exercise of my discretion deployed my platoon, pushing it forward at a run, with trailed arms, to strengthen the skirmish line, which I overtook some thirty or forty yards from the wood. Then—I can't describe it—the forest seemed all at once to flame up and disappear with a crash like that of a great wave upon the beach—a crash that expired in hot hissings, and the sickening "spat" of lead against flesh. A dozen of my brave fellows tumbled over like ten-pins. Some struggled to their feet, only to go down again, and yet again. Those who stood fired into the smoking brush and doggedly retired. We had expected to find, at most, a line of skirmishers similar to our own; it was with a view to overcoming them by a sudden *coup* at the moment of collision that I had thrown forward my little reserve. What we had found was a line of battle, coolly holding its fire till it could count our teeth. There was no more to be done but get back across the open ground, every superficial yard of which was throwing up its little jet of mud provoked by an impinging bullet. We got back, most of us, and I shall never forget the ludicrous incident of a young officer who had taken part in the affair walking up to his colonel, who had been a calm and apparently impartial spectator, and gravely reporting: "The enemy is in force just beyond this field, sir."

IX

In subordination to the design of this narrative, as defined by its title, the incidents related necessarily group themselves about my own personality as a center; and, as this center, during the few terrible hours of the engagement, maintained a variably constant relation to the open field already mentioned, it is important that the reader should bear in mind the topographical and tactical features of the local situation. The hither side of the field was occupied by the front of my brigade—a length of two regiments in line, with proper intervals for field batteries. During the entire fight the enemy held the slight wooded acclivity beyond. The debatable ground to the right and left of the open was broken and thickly wooded for miles, in some places quite inaccessible to artillery and at very few points offering opportunities for its successful employment. As a consequence of this the two sides of the field were soon studded thickly with confronting guns, which flamed away at one another with amazing zeal and rather startling effect. Of course, an infantry attack delivered from either side was not to be thought of when the covered flanks offered inducements so unquestionably superior; and I believe the riddled bodies of my poor skirmishers were the only ones left on this "neutral ground" that day. But there was a very pretty line of dead continually growing in our rear, and doubtless the enemy had at his back a similar encouragement.

The configuration of the ground offered us no protection. By lying flat on our faces between the guns we were screened from view by a straggling row of brambles, which marked the course of an obsolete fence; but the enemy's grape was sharper than his eyes, and it was poor consolation to know that his gunners could not see what they were doing, so long as they did it. The shock of our own pieces nearly deafened us, but in the brief intervals we could hear the battle roaring and stammering in the dark reaches of the forest to the right and left, where our other divisions were dashing themselves again and again into the smoking jungle. What would we not have given to join them in their brave, hopeless task! But to lie inglorious beneath showers of shrapnel darting divergent from the unassailable sky—meekly to be blown out of life by level gusts of grape—to clench our teeth and shrink helpless before big shot pushing noisily through the consenting air—this was horrible! "Lie down, there!" a captain would shout, and then get up himself to see that his order was obeyed. "Captain, take cover, sir!" the lieutenant-colonel would shriek, pacing up and down in the most exposed position that he could find.

O those cursed guns!—not the enemy's, but our own. Had it not been for them, we might have died like men. They must be supported, forsooth, the feeble, boasting bullies! It was impossible to conceive that these pieces were doing the enemy as excellent a mischief as his were doing us; they seemed to raise their "cloud by day" solely to direct aright the streaming procession of Confederate missiles. They no longer inspired confidence, but begot apprehension; and it was with grim satisfaction that I saw the carriage of one and another smashed into matchwood by a whooping shot and bundled out of the line.

X

The dense forests wholly or partly in which were fought so many battles of the Civil War, lay upon the earth in each autumn a thick deposit of dead leaves and stems, the decay of which forms a soil of surprising depth and richness. In dry weather the upper stratum is as inflammable as tinder. A fire once kindled in it will spread with a slow, persistent advance as far as local conditions permit, leaving a bed of light ashes beneath which the less combustible accretions of previous years will smolder until extinguished by rains. In many of the engagements of the war the fallen leaves took fire and roasted the fallen men. At Shiloh, during the first day's fighting, wide tracts of woodland were burned over in this way and scores of wounded who might have recovered perished in slow torture. I remember a deep ravine a little to the left and rear of the field I have described, in which, by some mad freak of heroic incompetence, a part of an Illinois regiment had been surrounded, and refusing to surrender was destroyed, as it very well deserved. My regiment having at last been relieved at the guns and moved over to the heights above this ravine for no obvious purpose, I obtained leave to go down into the valley of death and gratify a reprehensible curiosity.

Forbidding enough it was in every way. The fire had swept every superficial foot of it, and at every step I sank into ashes to the ankle. It had contained a thick undergrowth of young saplings, every one of which had been severed by a bullet, the foliage of the prostrate tops being afterward burnt and the stumps charred. Death had put his sickle into this thicket and fire had gleaned the field. Along a line which was not that of extreme depression, but was at every point significantly equidistant from the heights on either hand, lay the bodies, half buried in ashes; some in the unlovely looseness of attitude denoting sudden death by the bullet, but by far the greater number in postures of agony that told of the tormenting flame. Their clothing was half burnt away—their hair and beard entirely; the rain had come too late to save their nails. Some were swollen to double girth; others shriveled to manikins. According to degree of exposure, their faces were bloated and black or yellow and shrunken. The contraction of muscles which had given them claws for hands had cursed each countenance with a hideous grin. Faugh! I cannot catalogue the charms of these gallant gentlemen who had got what they enlisted for.

XI

It was now three o'clock in the afternoon, and raining. For fifteen hours we had been wet to the skin. Chilled, sleepy, hungry and disappointed—profoundly disgusted with the inglorious part to which they had been condemned—the men of my regiment did everything doggedly. The spirit had gone quite out of them. Blue sheets of powder smoke, drifting amongst the trees, settling against the hillsides and beaten into nothingness by the falling rain, filled the air with their peculiar pungent odor, but it no longer stimulated. For miles on either hand could be heard the hoarse murmur of the battle, breaking out near by with frightful distinctness, or sinking to a murmur in the distance; and the one sound aroused no more attention than the other.

We had been placed again in rear of those guns, but even they and their iron antagonists seemed to have tired of their feud, pounding away at one another with amiable infrequency. The right of the regiment extended a little beyond the field. On the prolongation of the line in that direction were some regiments of another division, with one in reserve. A third of a mile back lay the remnant of somebody's brigade looking to its wounds. The line of forest bounding this end of the field stretched as straight as a wall from the right of my regiment to Heaven knows what regiment of the enemy. There suddenly appeared, marching down along this wall, not more than two hundred yards in our front, a dozen files of gray-clad men with rifles on the right shoulder. At an interval of fifty yards they were followed by perhaps half as many more; and in fair supporting distance of these stalked with confident mien a single man! There seemed to me something indescribably ludicrous in the advance of this handful of men upon an army, albeit with their left flank protected by a forest. It does not so impress me now. They were the exposed flanks of three lines of infantry, each half a mile in length. In a moment our gunners had grappled with the nearest pieces, swung them half round, and were pouring streams of canister into the invaded wood. The infantry rose in masses, springing into line. Our threatened regiments stood like a wall, their loaded rifles at "ready," their bayonets hanging quietly in the scabbards. The right wing of my own regiment was thrown slightly backward to threaten the flank of the assault. The battered brigade away to the rear pulled itself together.

Then the storm burst. A great gray cloud seemed to spring out of the forest into the faces of the waiting battalions. It was received with a crash that made the very trees turn up their leaves. For one instant the assailants paused above their dead, then struggled forward, their bayonets glittering in the eyes that shone behind the smoke. One moment, and those unmoved men in blue would be impaled. What were they about? Why did they not fix bayonets? Were they stunned by their own volley? Their inaction was maddening! Another tremendous crash!—the rear rank had fired! Humanity, thank Heaven! is not made for this, and the shattered gray mass drew back a score of paces, opening a feeble fire. Lead had scored its old-time victory over steel; the heroic had broken its great heart against the commonplace. There are those who say that it is sometimes otherwise.

All this had taken but a minute of time, and now the second Confederate line swept down and poured in its fire. The line of blue staggered and gave way; in those two terrific volleys it seemed to have quite poured out its spirit. To this deadly work our reserve regiment now came up with a run. It was surprising to see it spitting fire with never a sound, for such was the infernal din that the ear could take in no more. This fearful scene was enacted within fifty paces of our toes, but we were rooted to the ground as if we had grown there. But now our commanding officer rode from behind us to the front, waved his hand with the courteous gesture that says *apres vous,* and with a barely audible cheer we sprang into the fight. Again the smoking front of gray receded, and again, as the enemy's third line emerged from its leafy covert, it pushed forward across the piles of dead and wounded to threaten with protruded steel.

Never was seen so striking a proof of the paramount importance of numbers. Within an area of three hundred yards by fifty there struggled for front places no fewer than six regiments; and the accession of each, after the first collision, had it not been immediately counterpoised, would have turned the scale.

As matters stood, we were now very evenly matched, and how long we might have held out God only knows. But all at once something appeared to have gone wrong with the enemy's left; our men had somewhere pierced his line. A moment later his whole front gave way, and springing forward with fixed bayonets we pushed him in utter confusion back to his original line. Here, among the tents from which Grant's people had been expelled the day before, our broken and disordered regiments inextricably intermingled, and drunken with the wine of triumph, dashed confidently against a pair of trim battalions, provoking a tempest of hissing lead that made us stagger under its very weight. The sharp onset of another against our flank sent us whirling back with fire at our heels and fresh foes in merciless pursuit—who in their turn were broken upon the front of the invalided brigade previously mentioned, which had moved up from the rear to assist in this lively work.

As we rallied to reform behind our beloved guns and noted the ridiculous brevity of our line—as we sank from sheer fatigue, and tried to moderate the terrific thumping of our hearts—as we caught our breath to ask who had seen such-and-such a comrade, and laughed hysterically at the reply—there swept past us and over us into the open field a long regiment with fixed bayonets and rifles on the right shoulder. Another followed, and another; two—three—four! Heavens! where do all these men come from, and why did they not come before? How grandly and confidently they go sweeping on like long blue waves of ocean chasing one another to the cruel rocks! Involuntarily we draw in our weary feet beneath us as we sit, ready to spring up and interpose our breasts when these gallant lines shall come back to us across the terrible field, and sift brokenly through among the trees with spouting fires at their backs. We still our breathing to catch the full grandeur of the volleys that are to tear them to shreds. Minute after minute passes and the sound does not come. Then for the first time we note that the silence of the whole region is not comparative, but absolute. Have we become stone deaf? See; here comes a stretcher-bearer, and there a surgeon! Good heavens! a chaplain!

The battle was indeed at an end.

XII

And this was, O so long ago! How they come back to me—dimly and brokenly, but with what a magic spell—those years of youth when I was soldiering! Again I hear the far warble of blown bugles. Again I see the tall, blue smoke of camp-fires ascending from the dim valleys of Wonderland. There steals upon my sense the ghost of an odor from pines that canopy the ambuscade. I feel upon my cheek the morning mist that shrouds the hostile camp unaware of its doom, and my blood stirs at the ringing rifle-shot of the solitary sentinel. Unfamiliar landscapes, glittering with sunshine or sullen with rain, come to me demanding recognition, pass, vanish and give place to others. Here in the night stretches a wide and blasted field studded with half-extinct fires burning redly with I know not what presage of evil. Again I shudder as I note its desolation and its awful silence. Where was it? To what monstrous inharmony of death was it the visible prelude?

O days when all the world was beautiful and strange; when unfamiliar constellations burned in the Southern midnights, and the mocking-bird poured out his heart in the moon-gilded magnolia; when there was something new under a new sun; will your fine, far memories ever cease to lay contrasting pictures athwart the harsher features of this later world, accentuating the ugliness of the longer and tamer life? Is it not strange that the phantoms of a blood-stained period have so airy a grace and look with so tender eyes?—that I recall with difficulty the danger and death and horrors of the time, and without effort all that was gracious and picturesque? Ah, Youth, there is no such wizard as thou! Give me but one touch of thine artist hand upon the dull canvas of the Present; gild for but one moment the drear and somber scenes of to-day, and I will willingly surrender an other life than the one that I should have thrown away at Shiloh.

Wit and Humor

If without the faculty of observation one could acquire a thorough knowledge of literature, the *art* of literature, one would be astonished to learn "by report divine" how few professional writers can distinguish between one kind of writing and another. The difference between description and narration, that between a thought and a feeling, between poetry and verse, and so forth—all this is commonly imperfectly understood, even by most of those who work fairly well by intuition.

The ignorance of this sort that is most general is that of the distinction between wit and humor, albeit a thousand times expounded by impartial observers having neither. Now, it will be found that, as a rule, a shoemaker knows calfskin from sole-leather and a blacksmith can tell you wherein forging a clevis differs from shoeing a horse. He will tell you that it is his business to know such things, so he knows them. Equally and manifestly it is a writer's business to know the difference between one kind of writing and another kind, but to writers generally that advantage seems to be denied: they deny it to themselves.

I was once asked by a rather famous author why we laugh at wit. I replied: "We don't—at least those of us who understand it do not." Wit may make us smile, or make us wince, but laughter—that is the cheaper price that we pay for an inferior entertainment, namely, humor. There are persons who will laugh at anything at which they think they are expected to laugh. Having been taught that anything funny is witty, these benighted persons naturally think that anything witty is funny.

Who but a clown would laugh at the maxims of Rochefoucauld, which are as witty as anything written? Take, for example, this hackneyed epigram: "There is something in the misfortunes of our friends which we find not entirely displeasing"—I translate from memory. It is an indictment of the whole human race; not altogether true and therefore not altogether dull, with just enough of audacity to startle and just enough of paradox to charm, profoundly wise, as bleak as steel—a piece of ideal wit, as admirable as a well cut grave or the headsman's precision of stroke, and about as funny.

Take Rabelais' saying that an empty stomach has no ears. How pitilessly it displays the primitive beast alurk in us all and moved to activity by our elemental disorders, such as the daily stress of hunger! Who could laugh at the horrible disclosure, yet who forbear to smile approval of the deftness with which the animal is unjungled?

In a matter of this kind it is easier to illustrate than to define. Humor (which is not inconsistent with pathos, so nearly allied are laughter and tears) is Charles Dickens; wit is Alexander Pope. Humor is Dogberry; wit is Mercutio. Humor is "Artemus Ward," "John Phoenix," "Josh Billings," "Petroleum V. Nasby," "Orpheus C. Kerr," "Bill" Nye, "Mark Twain"—their name is legion; for wit we must brave the perils of the deep: it is "made in France" and hardly bears transportation. Nearly all Americans are humorous; if any are born witty, Heaven help them to emigrate! You shall not meet an American and talk with him two minutes but he will say something humorous; in ten days he will say nothing witty; and if he did, your own, O most witty of all possible readers, would be the only ear that would give it recognition. Humor is tolerant, tender; its ridicule caresses. Wit stabs, begs pardon—and turns the weapon in the wound. Humor is a sweet wine, wit a dry; we know which is preferred by the connoisseur. They may be mixed, forming an acceptable blend. Even Dickens could on rare occasions blend them, as when he says of some solemn ass that his ears have reached a rumor.

My conviction is that while wit is a universal tongue (which few, however, can speak) humor is everywhere a *patois* not "understanded of the people" over the province border. The best part of it—its "essential spirit and uncarnate self," is indigenous, and will not flourish in a foreign soil. The humor of one race is in some degree unintelligible to another race, and even in transit between two branches of the same race loses something of its flavor. To the American mind, for example, nothing can be more dreary and dejecting than an English comic paper; yet there is no reason to doubt that *Punch* and *Judy* and the rest of them have done much to dispel the gloom of the Englishman's brumous environment and make him realize his relationship to Man.

It may be urged that the great English humorists are as much read in this country as in their own; that Dickens, for example, has long "ruled as his demesne" the country which had the unhappiness to kindle the fires of contempt in him and Rudyard Kipling; that "the excellent Mr. Twain" has a large following beyond the Atlantic. This is true enough, but I am convinced that while the American enjoys his Dickens with sincerity, the gladness of his soul is a tempered emotion compared with that which riots in the immortal part of John Bull when that singular instrument feels the touch of the same master. That a jest of Mark Twain ever got itself all inside the four corners of an English understanding is a proposition not lightly to be accepted without hearing counsel.

Thought and Feeling

"What is his idea?—what thought does he express?" asks—rather loftily—a distinguished critic and professor of English literature to whom I submitted a brief poem of Mr. Loveman. I had not known that Mr. Loveman (of whom, by the way, I have not heard so much as I expect to) had tried to express a thought; I had supposed that his aim was to produce an emotion, a feeling. That is all that a poet—as a poet—can do. He may be philosopher as well as poet—may have a thought, as profound a thought as you please, but if he do not express it so as to produce an emotion in an emotional mind he has not spoken as a poet speaks. It is the philosopher's trade to make us think, the poet's to make us feel. If he is so fortunate as to have his thought, well and good; he can make us feel, with it as well as without—and without it as well as with.

One would not care to give up the philosophy that underruns so much of Shakespeare's work, but how little its occasional absence affects our delight is shown by the reading of such "nonsense verses" as the song in "As You Like It," beginning:

It was a lover and his lass,
With a hey, and a ho, and a hey nonino.

One does not need the music; the lines sing themselves, and are full of the very spirit of poetry. What the dickens they may chance to mean is quite another matter. What is poetry, anyhow, but "glorious nonsense"? But how very glorious the nonsense happens to be! What "thought" did Ariel try to express in his songs in "The Tempest"? There is hardly the tenth part of a thought in them; yet who that has a rudimentary, or even a vestigial, susceptibility to sentiment and feeling, can read them without the thrill that is stubborn to the summoning of the profoundest reflections of Hamlet in his inkiest cloak?

Poetry may be conjoined with thought. In the great poets it commonly is—that is to say, we award the palm to him who is great in more than one direction. But the poetry is a thing apart from the thought and demanding a separate consideration. The two have no more essential connection than the temple and its granite, the statue and its bronze. Is the sculptor's work less great in the clay than it becomes in the hands of the foundry man?

No one, not the greatest poet nor the dullest critic, knows what poetry is. No man, from Milton down to the acutest and most pernicious lexicographer, has been able to define its name. To catch that butterfly the critic's net is not fine enough by much. Like electricity, it is felt, not known. If it could be known, if the secret were accessible to analysis, why, one could be taught to write poetry without having been "born unto singing."

So it happens that the most penetrating criticism must leave eternally unsaid the thing that is most worth saying. We can say of a poem as of a picture, an Ionic column, or any work of art: "It is charming!" But why and how it charms—there we are dumb, its creator no less than another.

What is it in art before which all but the unconscious peasant and the impenitent critic confess the futility of speech? Why does a certain disposition of words affect us deeply when if differently arranged to mean the same thing they stir no emotion whatever? He who can answer that has surprised the secret of the Sphinx, and after him shall be no more poetry forever!

Expound who is able the charm of these lines from "Kubla Khan:"

A damsel with a dulcimer
In a vision once I saw.
It was an Abyssinian maid,
And on her dulcimer she played,
Singing of Mount Abora.

There is no "thought" here—nothing but the baldest narrative in common words arranged in their natural order; but upon whose heart-strings does not that maiden play?—and who does not adore her?

Like the entire poem of which they are a part, and like the entire product of which the poem is a part, the lines are all imagination and emotion. They address, not the intellect, but the heart. Let the analyst of poetry wrestle with them if he is eager to be thrown.

To Train A Writer

There is a good deal of popular ignorance about writing; it is commonly thought that good writing comes of a natural gift and that without the gift the trick can not be turned. This is true of great writing, but not of good. Any one with good natural intelligence and a fair education can be taught to write well, as he can be taught to draw well, or play billiards well, or shoot a rifle well, and so forth; but to do any of these things greatly is another matter. If one can not do great work it is worth while to do good work and think it great.

I have had some small experience in teaching English composition, and some of my pupils are good enough to permit me to be rather proud of them. Some I have been able only to encourage, and a few will recall my efforts to profit them by dissuasion. I should not now think it worth while to teach a pupil to write merely well, but given one capable of writing greatly, and five years in which to train him, I should not permit him to put pen to paper for at least two of them—except to make notes. Those two years should be given to broadening and strengthening his mind, teaching him how to think and giving him something to think about—to sharpening his faculties of observation, dispelling his illusions and destroying his ideals. That would hurt: he would sometimes rebel, doubtless, and have to be subdued by a diet of bread and water and a poem on the return of our heroes from Santiago.

If I caught him reading a newly published book, save by way of penance, it would go hard with him. Of our modern education he should have enough to read the ancients: Plato, Aristotle, Marcus Aurelius, Seneca and that lot—custodians of most of what is worth knowing. He might retain what he could of the higher mathematics if he had been so prodigal of his time as to acquire any, and might learn enough of science to make him prefer poetry; but to learn from Euclid that the three angles of a triangle are equal to two right angles, yet not to learn from Epictetus how to be a worthy guest at the table of the gods, would be accounted a breach of contract.

But chiefly this fortunate youth with the brilliant future should learn to take comprehensive views, hold large convictions and make wide generalizations. He should, for example, forget that he is an American and remember that he is a Man. He should be neither Christian, nor Jew, nor Buddhist, nor Mahometan, nor Snake Worshiper. To local standards of right and wrong he should be civilly indifferent. In the virtues, so-called, he should discern only the rough notes of a general expediency; in fixed moral principles only time-saving predecisions of cases not yet before the court of conscience. Happiness should disclose itself to his enlarging intelligence as the end and purpose of life; art and love as the only means to happiness. He should free himself of all doctrines, theories, etiquettes, politics, simplifying his life and mind, attaining clarity with breadth and unity with height. To him a continent should not seem wide, nor a century long. And it would be needful that he know and have an ever present consciousness that this is a world of fools and rogues, blind with superstition, tormented with envy, consumed with vanity, selfish, false, cruel, cursed with illusions—frothing mad!

We learn in suffering what we teach in song—and prose. I should pray that my young pupil would occasionally go wrong, experiencing the educational advantages of remorse; that he would dally with some of the more biting vices. I should be greatly obliged if Fortune would lay upon him, now and then, a heavy affliction. A bereavement or two, for example, would be welcome, although I should not care to have a hand in it. He must have joy, too—O, a measureless exuberance of joy; and hate, and fear, hope, despair and love—love inexhaustible, a permanent provision. He must be a sinner and in turn a saint, a hero, a wretch. Experiences and emotions—these are necessaries of the literary life. To the great writer they are as indispensable as sun and air to the rose, or good, fat, edible vapors to toads. When my pupil should have had two years of this he would be permitted to try his 'prentice hand at a pig story in words of one syllable.

Aims and the Plan

(Preface to *Write It Right*)

The author's main purpose in this book is to teach precision in writing; and of good writing (which, essentially, is clear thinking made visible) precision is the point of capital concern. It is attained by choice of the word that accurately and adequately expresses what the writer has in mind, and by exclusion of that which either denotes or connotes something else. As Quintilian puts it, the writer should so write that his reader not only may, but must, understand.

Few words have more than one literal and serviceable meaning, however many metaphorical, derivative, related, or even unrelated, meanings lexicographers may think it worth while to gather from all sorts and conditions of men, with which to bloat their absurd and misleading dictionaries. This actual and serviceable meaning—not always determined by derivation, and seldom by popular usage—is the one affirmed, according to his light, by the author of this little manual of solecisms. Narrow etymons of the mere scholar and loose locutions of the ignorant are alike denied a standing.

The plan of the book is more illustrative than expository, the aim being to use the terms of etymology and syntax as little as is compatible with clarity, familiar example being more easily apprehended than technical precept. When both are employed the precept is commonly given after the example has prepared the student to apply it, not only to the matter in mind, but to similar matters not mentioned. Everything in quotation marks is to be understood as disapproved.

   Not all locutions blacklisted herein are always to be reprobated
as universal outlaws. Excepting in the case of capital offenders—
expressions ancestrally vulgar or irreclaimably degenerate—
absolute proscription is possible as to serious composition only; in
other forms the writer must rely on his sense of values and the fit-
ness of things. While it is true that some colloquialisms and, with
less of license, even some slang, may be sparingly employed in light
literature, for point, piquancy or any of the purposes of the skilled
writer sensible to the necessity and charm of keeping at least one
foot on the ground, to others the virtue of restraint may be commended as distinctly superior to the joy of indulgence.

   Precision is much, but not all; some words and phrases are disal-
lowed on the ground of taste. As there are neither standards nor
arbiters of taste, the book can do little more than reflect that of its
author, who is far indeed from professing impeccability. In neither taste nor precision is any man's practice a court of last appeal,
for writers all, both great and small, are habitual sinners against
the light; and their accuser is cheerfully aware that his own work
will supply (as in making this book it has supplied) many "awful
examples"—his later work less abundantly, he hopes, than his
earlier. He nevertheless believes that this does not disqualify him
for showing by other instances than his own how not to write.
The infallible teacher is still in the forest primeval, throwing
seeds to the white blackbirds.

Bierce on the Funding Bill

It is painful to observe that in his methods of affirming his right to the property of others, Mr. Huntington employs means not always justified by the end.

For a week past his daily contributions to the "Post" of this city have appeared in that honest journal as special telegrams from San Francisco, each duly dated the day before publication. Yet for three days or more of this week the dromedary head of Mr. Huntington, with its tandem bumps of cupidity and self-esteem overshadowing like twin peaks the organ that he is good with, in the valley between, has been more or less visible in the town. Indeed, the "Post's" distinguished special correspondent, with one leg in the grave, one arm in the Treasury and one eye on the police, has lighted the air with a dusky glimmer in all the dark corners of the Capitol, the dog-star of apprehension to all honest men and the sun of hope to Grove Johnson.

We have it on the best of authority that a man cannot be in two places at once unless he is a bird; so we are compelled to accept the painful conclusion from these premises that our friends, the telegraph companies, are none the richer for Mr. Huntington's connection with journalism. Indubitably he composes his San Franciscan dispatches in the shadow of the Capitol, already famous as the birthplace of Mr. Fleet Strother.

This inference is supported by other evidence that amounts to proof. There is in Washington, as elsewhere on this side of the continent, an acute public apathy regarding Mr. Huntington's methods, his aims, his accomplices and his cries for credit. The history of the crimes committed by him and his partners is almost unknown. Few persons one meets have a very definite knowledge of the Pacific Railroads, the enormous robberies connected with building and operating them, or the still greater robberies now in contemplation. To the general public here the various funding schemes now in discussion by a packed committee of the House are absolutely devoid of interest.

That a Washington newspaper should think it worth while to give columns of its space to the daily consideration of these matters for the entertainment or instruction of its readers is not conceivable without a mighty effort at making believe. The utmost concession that one can make with regard to the editor's good faith is that he prints the stuff at cut rates in deference to the poverty of a corporation that has yet much to steal.

There is also a significant similarity of literary style in the utterances of the thrifty Californian gentlemen quoted in these amazing works of the half human mind. It is as if some cunning hand had written the railroad's entire "case" on a continuous slip of paper, which had then been cut into lengths and each piece fitted with the name of some prominent citizen with a thoughtful pocket known to entertain kindly sentiments toward theft. This may not be the plan that was pursued, but certainly there is a charming uniformity of expression among these gentlemen who believe that a corporation which for thirty years has defaulted in the payment of interest and is about to default in the payment of principal because it has chosen to steal both principal and interest can henceforth be trusted to pay both.

These beads of personal opinion are strung upon a thread of editorial commentary satisfactorily strung in time to hold them from spilling. Some of these statements have a hardy audacity that makes a Californian gasp, though the majority of the House Committee on Pacific Railroads, to whom they are specially if not tacitly addressed, read and repeat them with lungs undisturbed. Here are a few of these pearls of thought, selected almost at random:

> *"The opinion in financial and commercial circles in San Francisco is overwhelmingly against the government taking the Pacific roads and operating them."*

"The financial and commercial community of San Francisco is somewhat alarmed lest Congress should think that the judgment of this city is in favor of government ownership of the Central Pacific Railroad."

"The effort to revive the rule of the sandlot is a dismal failure."

"Outside of a few disappointed agitators, the people favor an extension of the debt at a fair rate of interest."

"There are but a few people in the city outside of the sandlotters who are in favor of government ownership and operation of the Pacific Railroads."

"The opinion of all classes here is largely in favor of the Central Pacific funding bill."

All these monstrous statements, be it not forgotten, are made of San Francisco, whence these so-called telegrams profess to be sent. That they seem credible and true to those who have not special knowledge of the matter there is no reason to doubt. Their falsehood has been exposed in the committee by Representatives Bowers, Maguire and others, and will be exposed on the floors of both houses if ever the matter comes to a debate; but in the mean time it is having its natural effect elsewhere, despite the amusing fact that the other day an incorruptible linotype machine in the printing office of the "Post" dropped the honest words "Ad Pacific Railroads" in shooting capitals into the middle of one of Mr. Huntington's articles.

A Freak War

San Francisco Examiner, August 7, 1898

Of all wars concerning which we have knowledge—and history is mainly a narrative of wars—none has been distinguished by so many odd features as this of ours. Somebody has dubbed it the Yanko-Spanko war—a comical name which seems likely to stick for its apt and felicitous suggestion of something comical in the war itself. On examination we find this element easily "isolated," as Lewis Carroll's imagination isolated the grin of the cat, or, for a closer analogy, an even more daring fancy might detach that of a skull.

If in an opera bouffe the sovereign of Patagascar, moved by the sufferings of the oppressed people of Novagonis, whom their wicked rulers were starving, were to undertake the deliverance by a strict blockade of the country we should call it great fun. The notion of "starving out" the oppressors, with all the resources of the country at their command, in order to succor their landless and penniless victims, would nimbly and sweetly recommend itself unto our gentle sense of humor. Yet that is what (without a smile) we have done for the Cuban "reconcentrados," who made their moan to us, and to whose tale of woe we responded with a blockade. Truly we must be terrible indeed to our enemies if so fatal to our friends.

I have no disposition to criticize the blockade of Cuban ports as a military measure; it is both right and expedient and would in itself have been sufficient to effect the surrender of the entire island if the Spanish navy had been first destroyed in Spanish ports, or wherever found. But as a main incident of a "holy war" avowedly undertaken in the cause of humanity to break a famine in Cuba, it "goes neare to be fonny."

* * *

No less amusing (to our side) are some of the more spectacular scenes of our military extravaganza. In the first battle, when a dozen of the enemy's warships and hundreds of their crews were destroyed, not an American was killed. But the pranking gods who composed the piece were not utterly devoid of literary conscience: they mitigated the incredible disparity by so neat a touch of restraint as the wounding of a half-dozen victors by explosion of their own ammunition; the gods thereby securing something of the ludicrous effect natural to one's hoisting with one's own petard.

The most humorous feature of this battle is without a parallel in comic history: it reads like a narrative by Mark Twain or the late William Edgar Nye. After the American commander had battered the enemy's ships for several hours, and "had them going," he deliberately ceased firing and steamed out of range, greatly to the relief and joy of the opposition, who saw in the movement a confession of defeat. Alas for their hopes!—the "Yankee pigs" had merely gone to breakfast! After the refection they returned, picking their teeth, and made a finish of the fight. We are all proud of them, but they must excuse us if we laugh.

When the stage was set for the next great naval scene "the Master of the Show" had observed that in his topsey-turvey travesty of war he had gone too far—had transcended the decent limits of the possible; so he met the demands of artistic vraisemblance by solemnly providing that the victors should have one man killed. With this concession to realism the dead man's surviving seamates were so delighted that they raised a memorial fund for the widow. And now a movement is afoot to comfort the defeated Admiral for the loss of his men and ships by presenting him with a homestead in Florida!

* * *

At Santiago the naval operations were for several weeks confined to
terrific "bombardments," the horrible uproar being punctuated at
intervals by explosions of gun-cotton shells from the "Vesuvius."
Sometimes of a starless night this vessel would sneak up "close to"
and utter a brace of earthquakes against a hillside, or into the lone
waters of the harbor, or wherever it might please Providence to
direct them. For several hours the battleships bombarded the city
at a distance of five miles across a concealing mountain range, laying the guns by chart and compass and giving them elevation by
listing the ships. After several weeks of this terrible work (tremen-
dously applauded by the gallery) the place was taken by the army
and it was found that none of the defenses had been materially
injured by the bombardment, no guns had been dismounted,
nobody killed. "And the cat laughed."

The fighting about Santiago by the land forces was real enough
and tragic enough to satisfy the most exacting demand for something "bluggy," and Heaven send that we have no need of more of it;
but in one of its immediate results the "freak" character of the war
comes again into attention. The beleaguering army persuaded its
not very hard pressed enemy to yield by promising to send it to its
native land across the sea! If earlier in the campaign each man had
been promised in addition an acre of land and a mule "effusion of
blood" could probably have been prevented altogether. Doubtless it
is safer, cheaper and every way better to send Spaniards to Upper
Spain than to Lower—better even than to feed them as prisoners
until it shall please their Government to submit and end the war.
The inexpediency of it is not here affirmed; only the humor of it—
which if the reader fail to discover let him thank Heaven for a serious nature and pass on.

* * *

Another humorous feature of this merry war is seen in the grave,
not to say solemn, discussion of whether we shall keep or give away
the Philippine islands. For three months the entire nation has been
debating this question with engaging earnestness, without coming
to any conclusion, and the Administration is equally undecided. In

negotiating a peace it hesitates between retention and restoration, and with an intelligent eye upon the next Presidential election finally unloads the responsibility upon the unheeding shoulders of a commission. The fun of all this is that we can neither keep the islands nor give them up, for we have not yet been able to get possession of them. We hold just as much of them as is covered by the feet of our soldiers. Even the single city of Manila, lying beneath the guns of our fleet, we dare not take if able, for fear of provoking a rupture of our precarious relations with the insurgent army and the eight or ten millions of people behind them. The utmost that we can hope is such a shadowy title to these islands as we can compel Spain to give; actual possession is a matter of military operations extending over the lifetime of a generation and consuming hundreds of thousands of lives. Yet the debate on surrendering the Philippines or keeping them goes bravely on. I venture to suggest that if ambitious to promote hilarity in Heaven we can be equally entertaining by considering what we shall do with Mars and appointing a Governor-General of the Pleiades, with headquarters in the Lick Observatory.

* * *

In both Cuba and Philippina (the name is deferentially submitted) we are confronted with a possibility that is as droll as anything known to the stage. At Manila, indeed, it is more than a possibility: it has the imminence of a reasonable expectation. All signs foreshadow the necessity of an alliance with those whom we went to conquer, against those whom we went to aid. At Manila this amusing peril, though imminent is inevitable; by tact and patience we may put the hemlock from our lips; but in Cuba we shall almost certainly have to drain it with a constricted nose and a wry mouth. Nothing is more certain than that the Cuban insurgents are a minority and in the popular Government that we are pledged to set up will be outvoted and undone. That they will submit and "bow to the will of the people" is not to be expected: submission to the majority is to them unthinkable; of the will of the people they have never heard. They will indubitably take to the hills again and Gen. Weyler will not laugh alone at our efforts to find and subdue them.

* * *

It is a good war, and no American has cause to blush for our part in it. Some of even its drollest incidents have been singularly credible to us: for examples, our bloodless victories by sea and our magnanimity to the vanquished on land. In respect to that, indeed, we have made a record of which we may be justly proud. In fact, there has been on neither side much of that reasonless animosity and duncelike inability to be just which is war's ugliest characteristic. The traditional Spanish cruelty and treachery have not been in evidence—a fact most gratifying to those of us who hold that manner is an index to character—that gracious words and pleasing ways come of good hearts. True, they may be counterfeited by a rascal who is a good actor and ever attentive to the part that he is playing; but from such a thing as a whole nation of good actors Heaven has spared us, and, from highest to lowest, the Spaniards are a people of charming courtesy. The rudest and most illiterate of them will address another of his class, even his own wife, with a ceremonious yet simple civility, an aptness and delicacy of compliment and a natural dignity of delivery which are the envy and despair of our ruder race, imperfectly accessible to the contagion of refinement and signifying with coarser speech the sturdy brutality that subjugates the world. The Latin race has had its day. Despite certain savage "survivals" that mar its social life, it has carried personal refinement to a pitch incompatible with dominion in a world of "bloody noses and cracked crowns"; but in the sunset of its power its face is suffused with something of the glory of the transfiguration.

We can conquer these people without half trying, for we belong to the race of gluttons and drunkards to whom dominion is given over the abstemious. We are descendants and successors of the robber barons, the villeins and the carls of medieval days who, unlike in all else, felt the fellowship of drink and bloodshed—gorged themselves torpid upon roast boar, swilled mead out of cow's-horns until incapable, and after a swinish sleep overran a province or two by way of picking themselves up for another bout at the trenches and the tun. We are successors to the Berserkers, who fought all corners and all stayers, and drank themselves shivering drunk in every port of Europe. We are of the blood of the English, who with seventy thousand devotees of the great Belly God, to whom they offer abundant sacrifice of beef and grog, can hold in subjection and punish for infraction of their will two hundred and fifty millions of Asiatic vegetarians and teetotalers.

Yes, we can beat these soft spoken, temperate and picturesque Spaniards—beat them in boasting, beat them in swearing, beat them in battle and lie about them afterward as we did before—as during the period of our own civil dissensions we lied about one another. We can thrash them consummately and every day of the week, but we cannot understand them; and is it not a great golden truth, shining like a star, that what one does not understand one knows to be bad? Yet at the end of it all, when the clamor of battle is heard no more upon the hills and ocean no longer shivers from the shock of great guns, it may dawn upon us, slowly in the mild, dry light of a growing revelation, that the Spaniard is not so very bad a chap after all. And each elated American laying off his armor may perhaps hear and heed the still small voice of the conscience in his breast as it ventures to whisper: "And pray which of the saints are you?"

A Thumb-Nail Sketch

Many years ago I lived in Oakland, California. One day as I lounged in my lodging there was a gentle, hesitating rap at the door and, opening it, I found a young man, the youngest young man, it seemed to me, that I had ever confronted. His appearance, his attitude, his manner, his entire personality suggested extreme indifference. I did not ask him in, instate him in my better chair (I had two) and inquire how we could serve each other. If my memory is not at fault I merely said: "Well," and awaited the result.

"I am from the San Francisco *Examiner*," he explained in a voice like the fragrance of violets made audible, and backed a little away.

"O," I said, "you come from Mr. Hearst."

Then that unearthly child lifted its blue eyes and cooed: "I am Mr. Hearst."

His father had given him a daily newspaper and he had come to hire me to write for it. Twenty years of what his newspapers call "wage slavery" ensued, and although I had many a fight with his editors for my right to my self-respect, I cannot say that I ever found Mr. Hearst's chain a very heavy burden, though indubitably I suffered somewhat in social repute for wearing it.

If ever two men were born to be enemies he and I are they. Each stands for everything that is most disagreeable to the other, yet we never clashed. I never had the honor of his friendship and confidence, never was "employed about his person," and seldom entered the editorial offices of his newspapers. He did not once direct nor request me to write an opinion that I did not hold, and only two or three times suggested that I refrain for a season from expressing opinions that I did hold, when they were antagonistic to the policy of the paper, as they commonly were. During several weeks of a great labor strike in California, when mobs of ruffians stopped all railway trains, held the state capital and burned, plundered and murdered at will, he "laid me off," continuing, of course, my salary; and some years later, when striking employees of street railways were devastating St. Louis, pursuing women through the street and stripping them naked, he suggested that I "let up on that labor crowd." No other instances of "capitalistic arrogance" occur to memory. I do not know that any of his other writers enjoyed a similar liberty, or would have enjoyed it if they had had it. Most of them, indeed, seemed to think it honorable to write anything that they were expected to.

As to Mr. Hearst's own public writings, I fancy there are none: he could not write an advertisement for a lost dog. The articles that he signs and the speeches that he makes—well, if a man of brains is one who knows how to use the brains of others this amusing demagogue is nobody's dunce.

If asked to justify my long service to journals with whose policies I was not in agreement and whose character I loathed I should confess that possibly the easy nature of the service had something to do with it. As to the point of honor (as that is understood in the profession) the editors and managers always assured me that there was commercial profit in employing my rebellious pen; and I—O well, I persuaded myself that I could do most good by addressing those who had greatest need of me—the millions of readers to whom Mr. Hearst was a misleading light. Perhaps this was an erroneous view of the matter; anyhow I am not sorry that, discovering no preservative allowable under the pure food law that would enable him to keep his word overnight, I withdrew, and can now, without impropriety, speak my mind of him as freely as his generosity, sagacity or indifference once enabled me to do of his political and industrial doctrines, in his own papers.

In illustration of some of the better features of this man's strange and complex character let this incident suffice. Soon after the assassination of Governor Goebel of Kentucky—which seemed to me a particularly perilous "precedent" if unpunished—I wrote for one of Mr. Hearst's New York newspapers the following prophetic lines:

The bullet that pierced Goebel's breast
Can not be found in all the West.
Good reason: it is speeding here
To stretch McKinley on the bier

The lines took no attention, naturally, but twenty months afterward the President was shot by Czolgosz. Every one remembers what happened then to Mr. Hearst and his newspapers. His political enemies and business competitors were alert to their opportunity. The verses, variously garbled but mostly made into an editorial, or a news dispatch with a Washington date-line but usually no date, were published all over the country as evidence of Mr. Hearst's complicity in the crime. As such they adorned the editorial columns of the New York Sun and blazed upon a bill-board in front of Tammany Hall. So fierce was the popular flame to which they were the main fuel that thousands of copies of the Hearst papers were torn from the hands of newsboys and burned in the streets. Much of their advertising was withdrawn from them. Emissaries of the *Sun* overran the entire country persuading clubs, libraries and other patriot bodies to exclude them from the files. There was even an attempt made to induce Czolgosz to testify that he had been incited to his crime by reading them—ten thousand dollars for his family to be his reward; but this cheerful scheme was blocked by the trial judge, who had been informed of it. During all this carnival of sin I lay ill in Washington, unaware of it; and my name, although appended to all that I wrote, including the verses, was not, I am told, once mentioned. As to Mr. Hearst, I dare say he first saw the lines when all this hullabaloo directed his attention to them.

With the occurrences here related the incident was not exhausted. When Mr. Hearst was making his grotesque canvass for the Governorship of New York the Roosevelt Administration sent Secretary Root into the state to beat him. This high-minded gentleman incorporated one of the garbled prose versions of my prophecy into his speeches with notable effect and great satisfaction to his conscience. Still, I am steadfast in the conviction that God sees him; and if any one thinks that Mr. Root will not go to the devil it must be the devil himself, in whom, doubtless, the wish is father to the thought.

Hearst's newspapers had always been so unjust that no injustice could be done to them, and had been incredibly rancorous toward McKinley, but no doubt it was my luckless prophecy that cost him tens of thousands of dollars and a growing political prestige. For anything that I know (or care) they may have cost him his election. I have never mentioned the matter to him, nor—and this is what I have been coming to—has he ever mentioned it to me. I fancy there must be a human side to a man like that, even if he is a mischievous demagogue.

In matters of "industrial discontent" it has always been a standing order in the editorial offices of the Hearst newspapers to "take the side of the strikers" without inquiry or delay. Until the great publicist was bitten by political ambition and began to figure as a crazy candidate for office not a word of warning or rebuke to murderous mobs ever appeared in any column of his papers except my own. A typical instance of the falsification of news to serve a foul purpose may be cited here. In Pennsylvania, a ferocious mob of foreign miners armed with bludgeons marched upon the property of their employers, to destroy it, incidentally chasing out of their houses all the English-speaking residents along the way and clubbing all that they could catch. Arriving at the "works," they were confronted by a squad of deputy marshals, and while engaged in murdering the sheriff, who had stepped forward to read the riot act, were fired on and a couple of dozen of them killed. Naturally the deputy marshals were put on trial for their lives. Mr. Hearst sent my good friend Julius Chambers to report the court proceedings. Day after day he reported at great length the testimony (translated) of the saints and angels who had suffered the mischance "while peacefully parading on a public road." Then Mr. Chambers was ordered away and not a word of testimony for the defense (all in English) ever appeared in the paper.

Instances of such fair-mindedness as this could be multiplied by the thousand, but all, I charitably trust, have been recorded Elsewhere in a more notable Book than mine.

Never just, Mr. Hearst is always generous. He is not swift to redress a grievance of one of his employees against another, but he is likely to give the complainant a cottage, a steam launch, or a roll of bank notes, if that person happens to be the kind of man to accept it, and he commonly is. As to discharging anybody for inefficiency or dishonesty—no, indeed, not so long as there is a higher place for him. His notion of removal is promotion.

He once really did dismiss a managing editor, but in a few months the fellow was back in his old place. I ventured to express surprise. "Oh, that's all right," Mr. Hearst explained. "I have a new understanding with him. He is to steal only small sums hereafter; the large ones are to come to me."

In that incident we observe two dominant features in his character—his indifference to money and his marvelous sense of humor. He who should apprehend danger to public property from Mr. Hearst's elevation to high office would err. The money to which he is indifferent includes that of others, and he smiles at his own expense.

If there is a capable working newspaper man in this country who has not, *malgre lui*, a kindly feeling for Mr. Hearst, he needs the light. I do not know how it is elsewhere, but in San Francisco and New York Mr. Hearst's habit of having the cleverest (not, alas, the most conscientious) obtainable men, no matter what he had to pay them, advanced the salaries of all such men more than fifty percent. Possibly these have receded, and possibly the high average ability of his men has receded too—I don't know; but indubitably he did get the brightest men.

Some of them, I grieve to say, were imperfectly appreciative of their employer's gentle sway. At one time on the *Examiner* it was customary, when a reporter had a disagreeable assignment, for him to go away for a few days, then return and plead intoxication. That excused him. They used to tell of one clever fellow in whose behalf this plea was entered while he was still absent from duty. An hour afterward Mr. Hearst met him and, seeing that he was cold sober, reproved him for deceit. On the scamp's assurance that he had honestly intended to be drunk, but lacked the price, Mr. Hearst gave him enough money to re-establish his character for veracity and passed on.

I fancy things have changed a bit now, and that Mr. Hearst has changed with them. He is older and graver, is no longer immune to ambition, and may have discovered that good fellowship with his subordinates and gratification of his lone humor are not profitable in business and politics. Doubtless too, he has learned from observation of his entourage of sycophants and self-seekers that generosity and gratitude are virtues that have not a speaking acquaintance. It is worth something to learn that, and it costs something.

With many amiable and alluring qualities, among which is, or used to be, a personal modesty amounting to bashfulness, the man has not a friend in the world. Nor does he merit one, for, either congenitally or by induced perversity, he is inaccessible to the conception of an unselfish attachment or a disinterested motive. Silent and smiling, he moves among men, the loneliest man. Nobody but God loves him and he knows it; and God's love he values only in so far as he fancies that it may promote his amusing ambition to darken the door of the White House. As to that, I think that he would be about the kind of President that the country—daft with democracy and sick with sin—is beginning to deserve.

Sources

By Ambrose Bierce

Bierce, Ambrose. *The Collected Works of Ambrose Bierce*. 12 vols. New York: Neale Publishing, 1909–12.
———. *The Devil's Dictionary*. Intro. Roy Morris, Jr. New York: Oxford University Press, 1999.
———. *Write It Right: A Little Blacklist of Literary Faults*. New York: Neale Publishing, 1910.

Biographical and Literary Studies

Fatout, Paul. *Ambrose Bierce: The Devil's Lexicographer*. Norman: University of Oklahoma Press, 1951.
Grenander, M. E. *Ambrose Bierce*. New York: Twayne, 1971.
McWilliams, Carey. *Ambrose Bierce: A Biography*. New York: Albert & Charles Boni, 1929.
Morris, Roy Jr. *Ambrose Bierce: Alone in Bad Company*. New York: Oxford University Press, 1995.
Neale, Walter. *Life of Ambrose Bierce*. New York: Neale Publishing, 1929; rpt. New York: AMS Press, 1969.

Edited Collections

Berkove, Lawrence I., ed. *Skepticism and Dissent: Selected Journalism [of Bierce], 1898–1901*. Ann Arbor: UMI Research, 1986.
Fadiman, Clifton, ed. *The Collected Writings of Ambrose Bierce*. New York: Citadel, 1946.
Grenander, M.E., ed. *Poems of Ambrose Bierce*. Lincoln: University of Nebraska Press, 1995.
Hopkins, Ernest Jerome, ed. *The Complete Short Stories of Ambrose Bierce*. Lincoln: University of Nebraska Press, 1970.
Joshi, S. T., and David E. Schultz, eds. *A Much Misunderstood Man: Selected Letters of Ambrose Bierce*. Columbus: Ohio State University Press, 2003.
———. *A Sole Survivor: Bits of Autobiography [by Ambrose Bierce]*. Knoxville: University of Tennessee Press, 1998.
Pope, Bertha Clark, ed. *The Letters of Ambrose Bierce*. San Francisco: Book Club of California, 1922; rpt. New York: Gordian, 1967.

Major Works by Ambrose Bierce

At the urging of his publisher, Walter Neale, Bierce compiled his twelve-volume *Collected Works* from 1909 to 1912. The results of his prodigious efforts have been a mixed blessing for Bierce scholars: a strange concatenation of superior material and borderline dreck. Although the *Collected Works* happily brought together earlier Bierce collections long out of print, most of his best journalism and almost a third of his stories are missing from the twelve-volume *CW*. The dating of the entries is erratic, and it seems never to have occurred to Bierce that future generations would care about his often evocative personal correspondence. Listed below are the titles of each volume, with some brief indication of content.

I.   *Ashes of the Beacon* (prose satire and scraps of autobiography)
II.   *In the Midst of Life* (stories: 26 "Tales of Soldiers and Civilians")
III.   *Can Such Things Be?* (stories: 42 tales of horror and war)
IV.   *Shapes of Clay* (poems)
V.   *Black Beetles in Amber* (satiric verse)
VI.   *The Monk and the Hangman's Daughter* (reworked translation of a German story; fables)
VII.   *The Devil's Dictionary* (includes Preface reprinted in this anthology)
VIII. *Negligible Tales* (not all "negligible"); On with the Dance (satiric prose); Epigrams
IX.   *Tangential Views* (essays)
X.   *The Opinionator* (essays)
XI.   *Antepenultima* (essays)
XII.   *In Motley* (fables; satiric prose)

About the Editor

John R. Dunlap has taught for more than thirty years in the Department of Classics at Santa Clara University, where he offers courses in Latin, Greek, classical civilization, linguistics, and writing. Born in Palo Alto in 1945, he took a B.A. in English and Greek at Santa Clara University in 1968, pursued classical studies at Duke University, and, after a two-year stint in the U.S. Army, took an M.A. in linguistics at the University of Minnesota in 1975. The author of more than seventy articles and reviews, he lives in San Jose, California, with his wife, Victoria, and with Nathan and Anna, the two younger of their four children. The two older ones, David and Benjamin, live in southern California with their wives, busily producing grandchildren.

A California Legacy Book

Santa Clara University and Heyday Books are pleased to publish the California Legacy series, vibrant and relevant writings drawn from California's past and present.

Santa Clara University—founded in 1851 on the site of the eighth of California's original twenty-one missions—is the oldest institution of higher learning in the state. A Jesuit institution, it is particularly aware of its contribution to California's cultural heritage and its responsibility to preserve and celebrate that heritage.

Heyday Books, founded in 1974, specializes in critically acclaimed books on California literature, history, natural history, and ethnic studies.

Books in the California Legacy series appear as anthologies, single author collections, reprints of important books, and original works. Taken together, these volumes bring readers a new perspective on California's cultural life, a perspective that honors diversity and finds great pleasure in the eloquence of human expression.

Series editor: Terry Beers
Publisher: Malcolm Margolin
Advisory committee: Stephen Becker, William Deverell, Charles Faulhaber, David Fine, Steven Gilbar, Ron Hansen, Gerald Haslam, Robert Hass, Jack Hicks, Timothy Hodson, James Houston, Jeanne Wakatsuki Houston, Maxine Hong Kingston, Frank LaPena, Ursula K. Le Guin, Jeff Lustig, Tillie Olsen, Ishmael Reed, Alan Rosenus, Robert Senkewicz, Gary Snyder, Kevin Starr, Richard Walker, Alice Waters, Jennifer Watts, Al Young.

Thanks to the English Department at Santa Clara University and to Regis McKenna for their support of the California Legacy series.

CALIFORNIA
LEGACY

Other California Legacy Books

And many more!

If you would like to be added to the California Legacy mailing list, please send your name, address, phone number, and email address to:

California Legacy Project
English Department
Santa Clara University
Santa Clara, CA 95053

For more on California Legacy titles, events, or other information, please visit www.californialegacy.org.

HEYDAY INSTITUTE

Since its founding in 1974, Heyday Books has occupied a unique niche in the publishing world, specializing in books that foster an understanding of the history, literature, art, environment, social issues, and culture of California and the West. We are a 501(c)(3) nonprofit organization based in Berkeley, California, serving a wide range of people and audiences.

We are grateful for the generous funding we've received for our publications and programs during the past year from foundations and more than 300 individual donors. Major supporters include:

Anonymous; Anthony Andreas, Jr.; Barnes & Noble bookstores; BayTree Fund; S. D. Bechtel, Jr. Foundation; Fred & Jean Berensmeier; Butler Koshland Fund; California Council for the Humanities; Candelaria Fund; Columbia Foundation; Compton Foundation, Inc.; Federated Indians of Graton Rancheria; Wallace Alexander Gerbode Foundation; Marion E. Greene; Walter & Elise Haas Fund; Hopland Band of Pomo Indians; James Irvine Foundation; George Frederick Jewett Foundation; Guy Lampard & Suzanne Badenhoop; LEF Foundation; Michael McCone; Middletown Rancheria Tribal Council; National Audubon Society; National Endowment for the Arts; National Park Service; Philanthropic Ventures Foundation; Poets & Writers; Rim of the World Interpretive Association; River Rock Casino; Riverside-Corona Resource Conservation; Alan Rosenus; San Francisco Foundation; Santa Ana Watershed Association; William Saroyan Foundation; Sandy Cold Shapero; Service Plus Credit Union; L. J. Skaggs and Mary C. Skaggs Foundation; Swinerton Family Fund; Victorian Alliance; Tom White; and the Harold & Alma White Memorial Fund.

For more information about Heyday Institute, our publications and programs, please visit our website at www.heydaybooks.com.